Legend:
Horror Hospital Unplugged
By Dennis Cooper and Keith Mayerson
KEITH MAYERSON
HORROR
HOSPITAL
UNPLUGGED
CLICK HERE
Yes!
FINALLY VE GOTS HIM VER VE VANT HIM
I BRAKE FOR METEORITES
HORROR HOSPITAL
UNPLUGGED
NOT A CRUCIFIX BUT A TELEPHONE POLE
TEEN AGE SUPERSTAR
SATAN
I'M A BIG EXPLOSION
SHEEP

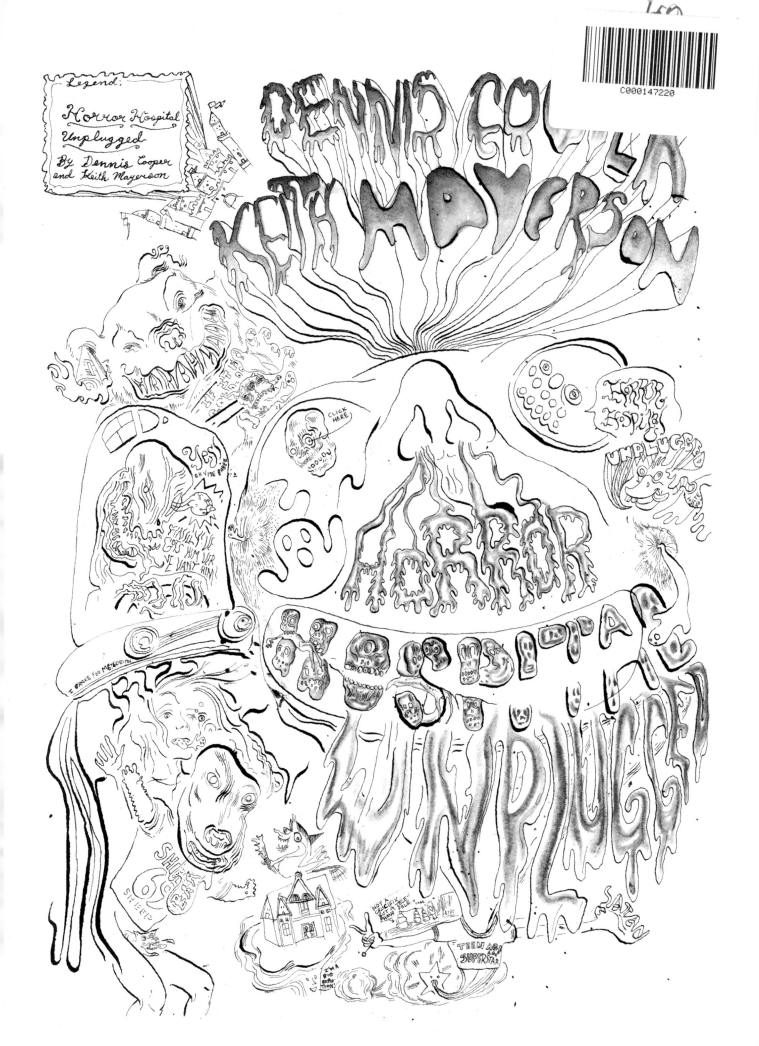

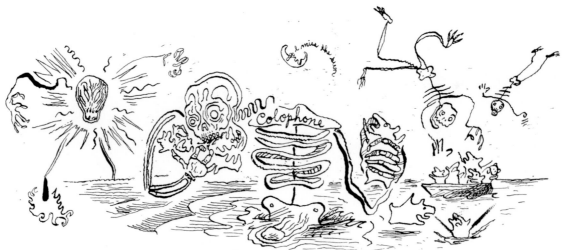

The producers of the contents that heresofor lieth before thee would life to gratefully (albiet humbly) thank thy personhood for whom we thank thine and theirs: Ira Silverberg, Andrea Juno, and Joel Westendorf for Dennis, and for Keith: his family and Andrew Madrid, who is his hunney-bunney.

The producers would also life to remind you, our dear reader, that any passing or otherwise resemblence or charactevs of any persons or aliens is a mere and simple coincidence, except in the case (s) in which we meant it, in which case this work suddenly becomes the work of satire, and is not meant to truly convey the sexual orientation, desires, musical abilities, talents, drug habits, or charactors of the characters portrayed herein. The artist would also like to acknowledge the memory of Jack Kirby, Wallace Wood, Peter Arno, Osamu Tezuka, and Antoine de Saint-Exupery, who, although dead, lent their talents to this project through their inspiration and providing key elements appropriated in their homage and because they are cool. Other key players provided inspiration but they are too numerous to mention so I wont mention ~~so I won't mention~~ them here. Questions or comments? Keiboy @ aol.com., tough guy.

This comic is presented solely as a visual fantasy. Some cautionary precaution taken by the producers may have been omitted due to editorial consideration, but all the performers praticed their ~~an999~~ ~~saf~~ sex safely, as should you.

All performers are 18 years of age or older. Proof of age on file.

Copyright © 1996 by Dennis Cooper and Keith Mayerson
ISBN: 0-9651042-1-4

Cooper, Dennis, 1953-
    Horror hospital unplugged / by Dennis Cooper and Keith Mayerson.
        p.   cm.
    ISBN 0-9651042-1-4 (pbk.)
    I. Mayerson, Keith, 1966- . II. Title.
    PN6727.C63H67 1996
    741.5'973--dc20

96-26240
CIP

BOOKSTORE DISTRIBUTION:
    U.S.: Consortium Book Sales and Distribution, 1045 Westgate Dr., Saint Paul, MN 55114-1065;
        toll free: 1-800-283-3572, tel.: (612) 221-9035, fax (612) 221-0124.
    UK & EUROPE: Airlift Book Co., 8 The Arena, Mollison Ave., Enfield Middlesex, ENGLAND EN3-7NJ;
        tel.: 181-804-0400, fax: 181-804-0044.
    AUSTRALIA & NEW ZEALAND: Peribo Pty Ltd, 58 Beaumont Rd., Mount Kuring-gai, NSW 2080,
        AUSTRALIA; tel.: 61-2-457-0011, fax: 61-2-457-0022.

For a catalog, send SASE to:
    Juno Books, 180 Varick St., 10th Floor, New York, NY 10014; tel.: (212) 807-7300, fax: (212) 807-7355.

First edition printed in Germany.

10 9 8 7 6 5 4 3 2 1

Cover art by Keith Mayerson.

HIS EYEBALL ON FIRE
COMING OUT OF EYE BALL
LEIF GARRETT
Now I'm Seal!
I'M THE WORLD'S FIRST MELTIN GARG OYLE
VISIT MY WEB SITE
IT'S OVAH
It's Time for
MOON PIE
OH MY GOD! LOOK LOOK KIDS ITS YOGA! YOGA FROM STAR BORES!
Let me come in your mouth
I have been WAITING FOR
FINALLY IT'S HERE!
ALL THIS TIME!
HEY there young fello I'M CAP'N CRUNCH!
A BOTTECHELLI ZITI SHELL
OH GRAY ALIEN- YOU FILET ME!
HOW DO YOU TUNA FISH? YOU PUT TULIPS ON HIS ORGAN
The Official
UNPLUGGED
TO READ MORE ABOUT
WAILS CLICK HERE
CHILLS CLICK HERE
PILLS CLICK HERE
MIRTH CLICK HERE
DEARTH CLICK HERE
RAYMOND BURR CLICK HERE
BLINKY CLICK HERE
ZEE ZO CLICK HERE
RIDOLIN CLICK HERE
I'M ORKAN DEFEATER OF EVIL & INJUSTICE!
YIP!
TABLE OF CONTENTS:
CHAPTER ONE: THE UNBEARABLE LIGHTWEIGHTINESS OF HORROR HOSPITAL
CHAPTER TWO: AOXOMOXOA
CHAPTER THREE: THE 120 MINUTES OF SODOM
CHAPTER FOUR? L'APPARITION IVRE
CHAPTER FIVE: THE BIBLE, PART II
TYPE YOUR MEMO HERE
THIS SPACE IS YOUR SPACE. DO ANYTHING YOU WANT IN IT.
OH YEAH AND THE OTHER THING
(EXCEPT THAT)

THE UNBEARABLE LIGHTWEIGHTINESS OF
HORROR HOSPITAL

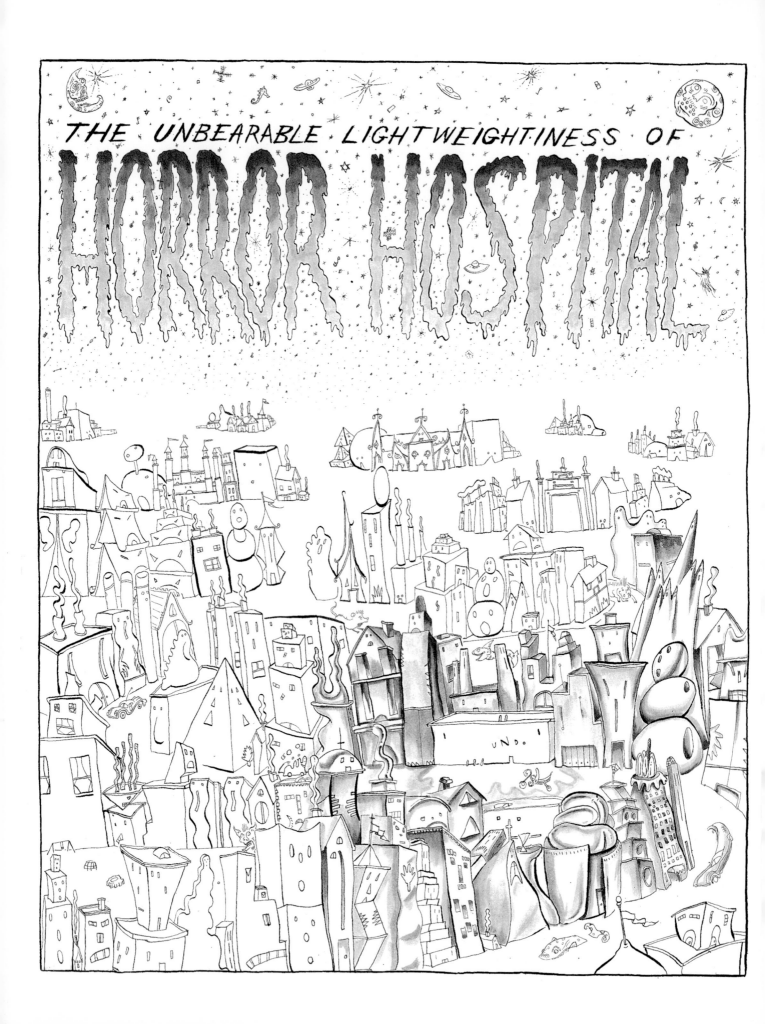

UNDO

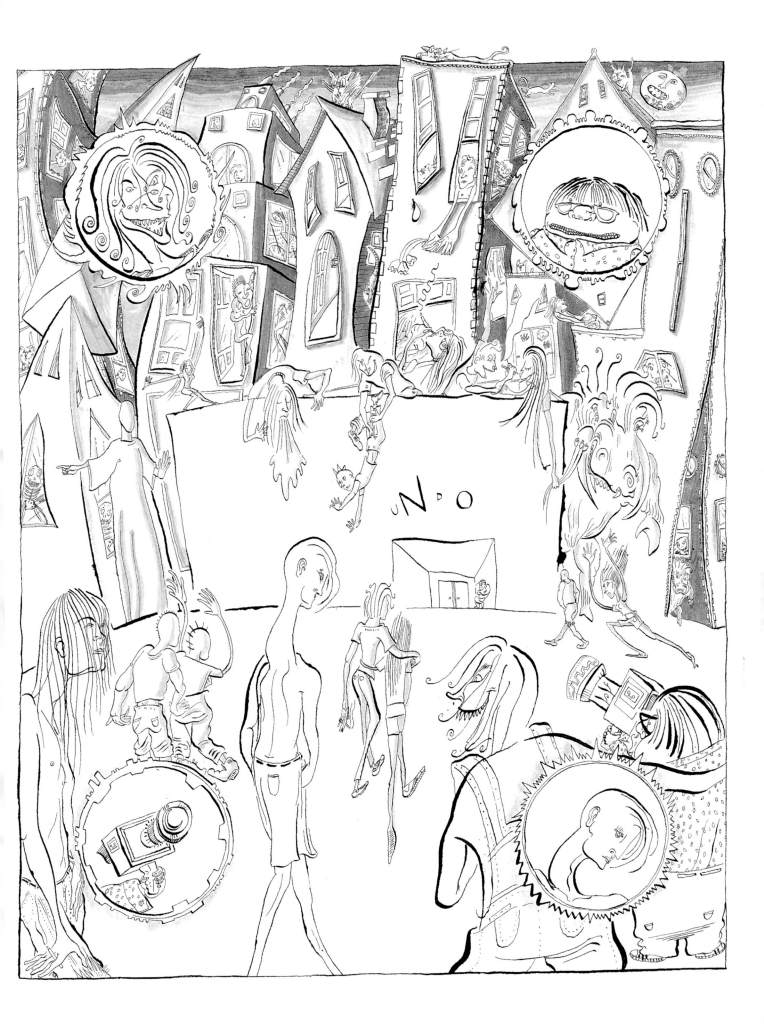

two...
e gods.
Really? Where?
FAT Bitch
BOO
ALEKA'S ATTIC!
Aleka's Attick!
FATSO

UNDO
Welcome to the world-ignored UNDO!
Aleko's Attic will be on soon. But first - here they are - from Reseda...
FATSO
BOO
BOO

HORROR HOSPITAL
HORROR HOSPITAL
HORROR HOSPITAL

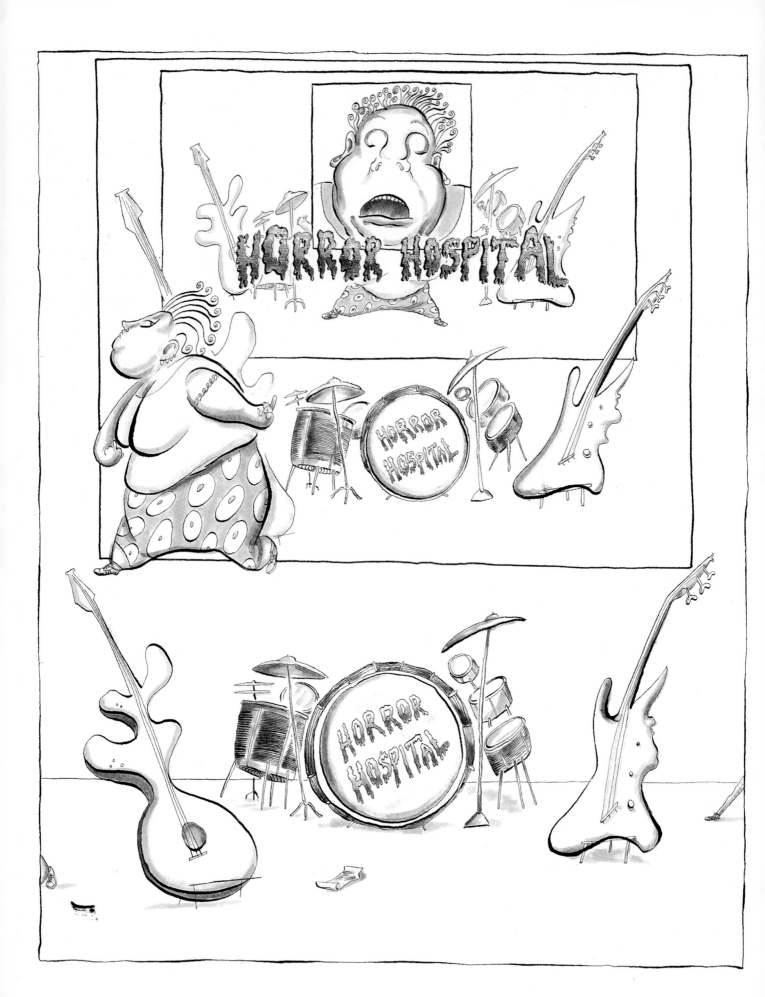

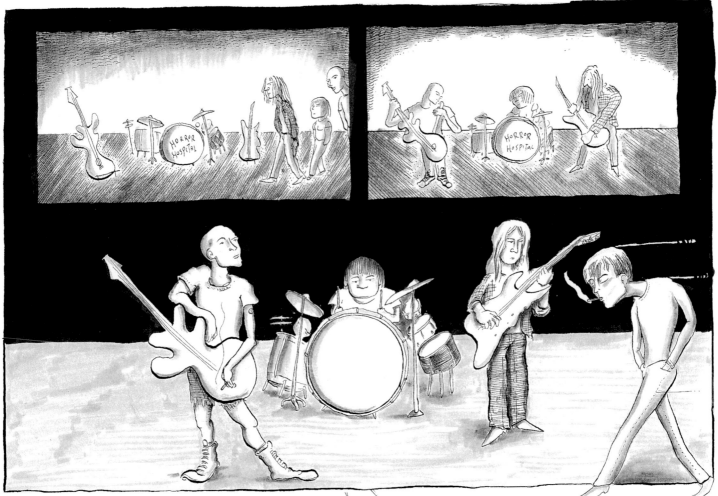

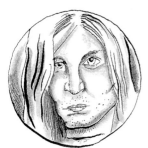

DULL
guitars

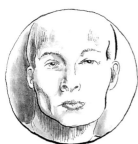

DEVAN
bass

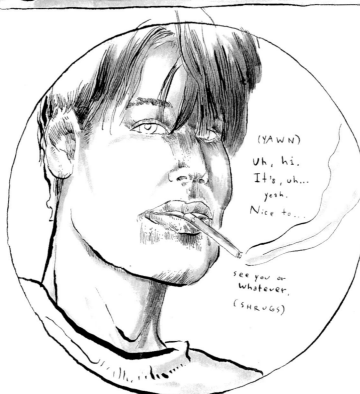

(YAWN)
Uh, hi.
It's, uh...
yeah.
Nice to...

see you or
whatever.
(SHRUGS)

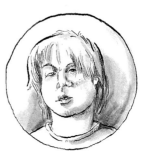

KIMBERLY
drums

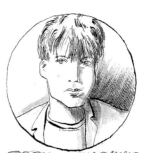

TREVOR MACHINE
voice

ONE! TWO! THREE!
CLACK CLACK CLACK
HORROR HOSPITAL
FUCK DEAD PEOPLE!
I DON'T KNOWWWW
THEY WON'T KNOWWWWW
THEY'RE COOL
IT'S HOT
WHY NOT?

God...
12.19.93
10:47
What did you say?
HORROR HOSPITAL
10:48
I said the singer's UNBELIEVABLE.
DYKE POWER
STYX
Yeah, they're interesting. Concise, mock-chaotic, nicely investing a punk historical referent with a kind of manic artificiality.

HUNH?

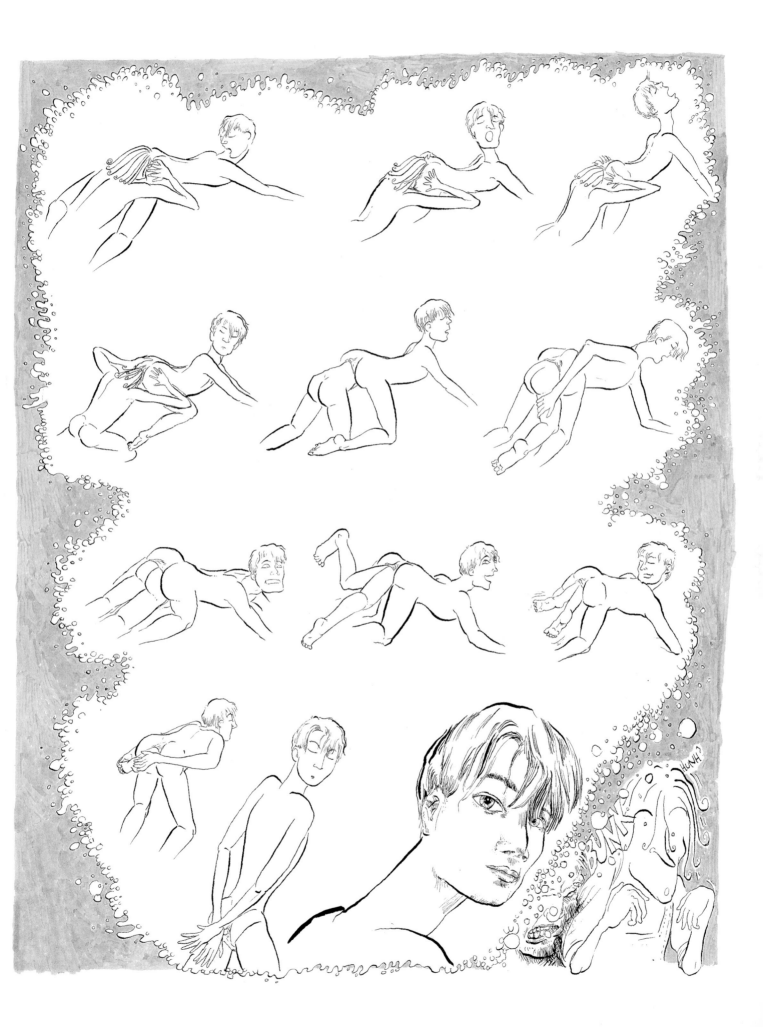

PATHETIC NEANDERTHAL!
BORN TO MOSH
clap cough clap
uh, okay.
yeah
uh..
well
Clap cough clap
this is one you'll probably like better.
HEY WAIT!
I DON'T CARE IF YOU LIKE IT OR NOT!
FUCKHEADS.
ONE
TWO
THREE!
You know, I think I'll intercut this footage with scenes from woodstock to show how concert behavior differs from generation to generation yet remains the same.
BRILLIANT, FRANK.

NOBODY KNOWS
AND I DON'T CARE
I'M A SUICIDE
IN A CARTOON WORLD
I'M A ROADRUNNER
I DIE AND DIE AND DIE
NEVER TO LIVE
FORTY MINUTES LATER...
THANKS, GOODNIGHT!
AND GOOD RIDDANCE!
WOOF WOOF
CLAP CLAP CLAP CLAP
?
BOO!
YOU SUCK
WASH ME
I DEDICATE OUR SET TO THIS GUY DOWN HERE. AND THE REST OF YOU, GO BACK TO LOLLAPALOOZA OR WHEREVER.
TEN MINUTES LATER
WE SERVICE MINORS
KFC

Our Fan.
You were magnificent
Oh RIGHT. Sure.
No REALLY. A STAR IS BORN, etcetera
Look...
uh... I just have to ask, okay? Are you, like making fun of me? 'Cos I don't have my contacts in and I can't tell.
Handshaking is kind of, uh, bourgeois, but...
What's your name

TREVOR MACHINE.
I'M DOUG, UH... WASTED.
COOL NAME.
OKAY, THIS IS THE LAST TIME I'LL ASK YOU SOMETHING LIKE THIS, I PROMISE, BUT, UH... LIKE I SAID, I DON'T HAVE MY CONTACTS IN, SO... IT'S HARD TO TELL, BUT... ARE YOU, UH... UH... LOOKING AT ME IN THE WAY IT SEEMS LIKE YOU'RE LOOKING AT ME? DO YOU KNOW WHAT I'M SAYING? 'COS... I MIGHT BE SORT OF FEELING THE SAME WAY ABOUT YOU, IF YOU ARE. BUT IF YOU AREN'T, THAT'S COOL TOO. AND I'M NOT SURE I'M QUEER ANYWAY, 'COS, UH, I'M AN INDIVIDUAL, YOU KNOW, AND NOT A, UH,... CATEGORY...
COME ON, HELP ME OUT UH... DOUG.
CAN I HAVE YOUR PHONE NUMBER?
YEAH, YEAH, OF COURSE. SHIT.
UH....

The NEXT DAY
FRANK'S PLACE
CRASS
Spandau Ballet
DON'T
RAP RAP
TAT TAT TAT
KISS
FRANK CALIFORNIA
DISTURBED
CRUSTY
BLAMANGE
MORRISEY RULES!
HEY SAILOR
BOWIE
STAR WARS
CURE
BLOOP!
DUH, DUH, DUH.... DU-U-U-UH.

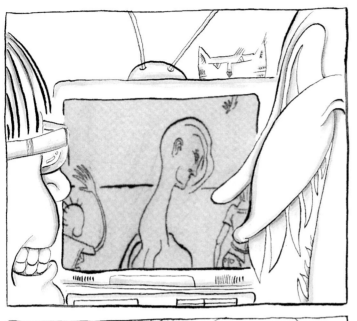

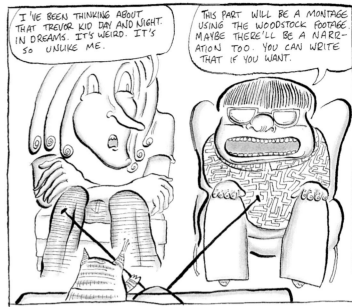

I'VE BEEN THINKING ABOUT THAT TREVOR KID DAY AND NIGHT. IN DREAMS. IT'S WEIRD. IT'S SO UNLIKE ME.

THIS PART WILL BE A MONTAGE USING THE WOODSTOCK FOOTAGE. MAYBE THERE'LL BE A NARRATION TOO. YOU CAN WRITE THAT IF YOU WANT.

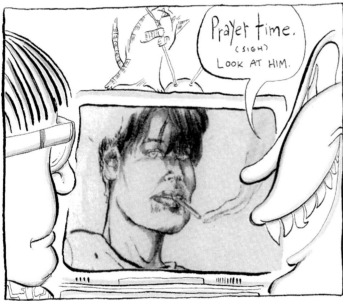

Prayer time.
(SIGH)
LOOK AT HIM.

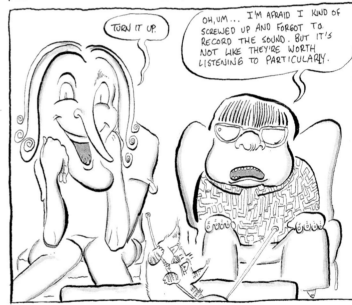

TURN IT UP.

OH, UM... I'M AFRAID I KIND OF SCREWED UP AND FORGOT TO RECORD THE SOUND. BUT IT'S NOT LIKE THEY'RE WORTH LISTENING TO PARTICULARLY.

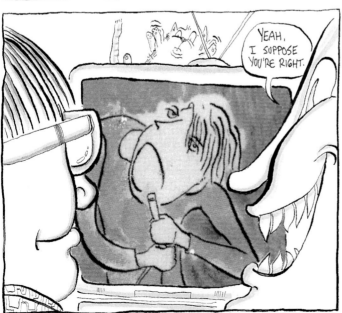

YEAH, I SUPPOSE YOU'RE RIGHT.

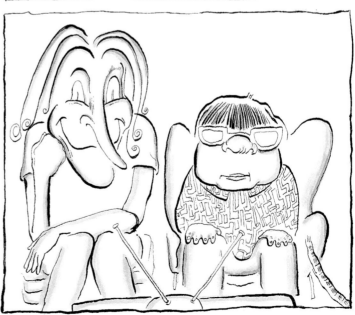

ACTUALLY, I THOUGHT I MIGHT PUT IN SOME WHITE NOISE. OR... MAYBE 'LISTEN TO THE MOCKINGBIRD.'

DID I EVER PLAY YOU THIS HILARIOUS VERSION I HAVE BY LAWRENCE WELK?

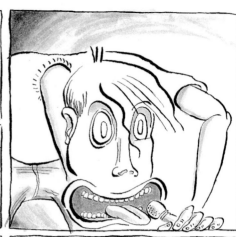

THE KID'S CUTE, DOUG, BUT YOU HAVE TO ADMIT HE'S KIND OF A JOKE. SORT OF A... PERRY FARREL WAN— NABE WHO'S ACTUALLY MORE LIKE A JOE COCKER WANNABE. YOU KNOW, LIKE WHEN JOE COCKER USED TO ACT All SPAZZY WHILE HE SANG?

OKAY, HE'S NOT A GOD. BUT HE'S INCREDIBLY FUCKABLE.

HE'S GOT A GREAT HOUR, MAYBE EVEN A GREAT HOUR-AND-A-HALF OF SEX IN HIM.

YOU HAVE TO ADMIT, HE'D LOOK PRETTY SCRUMPTIOUS IN HANDCUFFS.

MAYBE IF HIS MOUTH WAS TAPED SHUT.

THE BRAIN POSITIVELY SWIMS.

SIT UP, DOUG! COME ON, YOU SAID YOU'D WATCH MY VIDEO!

7 ELEVEN
YOU GET LOTSA' LIQUID FOR LESS IN OUR HUBBA HUBBA
SAUCE 98¢ MOOGLE
BAND 7.99 AIDS
NEW! WOOGLE 3.99
POOGLE! 4.62
RIP DOODLENOODLE 3.99 87
WARNING DO NOT PLAY ON OR AROUND
EMBER YOUR HUBBA
Del Taco
SPACE INVADER
AUTO TRADER
BEAT UP YOUR CHILD
RICE
DICE
LICE
MICE
Beat up your
BOO
FRANKENBOO
COUNT CHOCULA
REDBOOK
BEANBERRY
BERRYBERRY
HUNKYBERRY
JUJUBERRY
COSMO
SMOKE PENI CIGARET
LOTTO
PLAY TO WIN!
SLURPITUP!
EAT ME
BEAT UP YOUR CHILD
Los Angeles Times
COUNT CHOCULA
HEY! WHAT ABOUT HUBBA
Kill Your Parents
INSANE SEX TORTURE
LIPOSUCTION FOR BEGINNERS
RUBBING

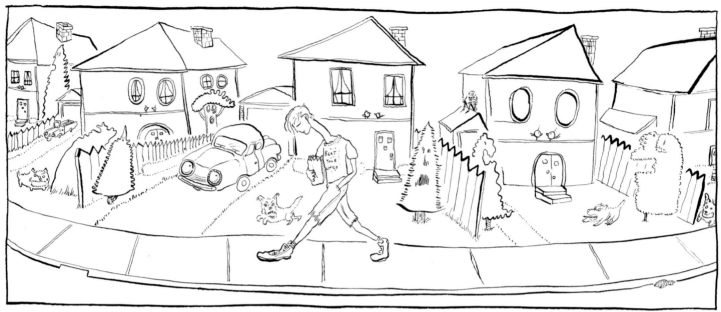

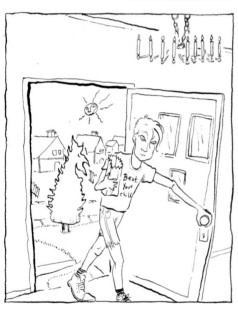

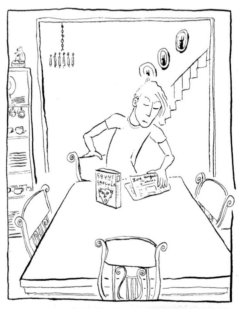

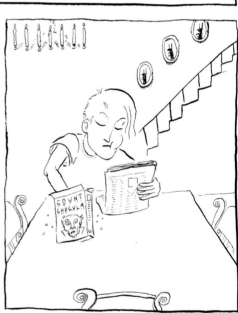

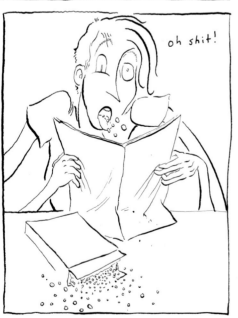

oh shit!

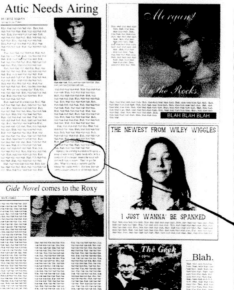

Attic Needs Airing

Gide Novel comes to the Roxy

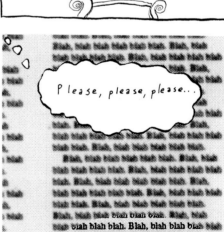

Please, please, please...

Opening the evening was Horror Hospital, a troop of very young floppy heads who, with a modicum of technique, treated the usual subjects with typical sneers. They've got the idea. What they need is maturity and the finesse that comes with it. For now their sincerity's almost a reason to sit through them.

RING RING!
uh... Oh, sorry, hello?
Is Trevor there?
Yeah. I mean, Hi.
This is Doug. I met you the other night.
Oh yeah. Hi. Hey, this is good timing. You can help me interpret something.
There's a review in the paper today of our show? And it says that, uh, we weren't that good technically, but
but we're sincere and so, 'cos of that, we're worth seeing...
uh huh.
So that's a compliment, right? 'Cos sincerity is more important than, uh, proficiency, right? I mean, that's a proven fact, isn't it?
Sure.
What are you up to right now?
nothing.
But, uh... So I should be happy about the review, right?
Definitely.
I'll come and pick you up. Where do you live?
AWESOME!

and I'm the goddamn moon 'cause it's night!
I'M the goddamn ocean!
BUILDINGS
CAPITAL RECORDS
HOLLYWOODLAWN
CORRUPTION
Chateau Monster
PARK IT IN THE REAR
WOW.
Doug
Fuck you I'M Bullwinkle!
TREVOR is very DRUNK & high!
Beat yer child
DEATH

PLEASE COLOR AT YOUR CONVENIENCE

So... uh, shit, What was I... saying?
Oh right. Yeah.
First, I write the lyrics.
I'm always stoned.
two joints usually does it.
SCOTCH
Then Dull and Devan put them to music.
I guess that sort of sounds kind of, uh, traditional
BOOZE
but...
meat
tongue

HOLLYWOOD
WOW.
Yeah, it's cool. So your friend, uh...
Yeah Yeah Yeah baby Yeah
Frank.
...yeah, Frank.
I'm an ALLIGATOR
...He really Wants to make a documentary about Horror Hospital?
Sure. Here, take one more of these...
SCOTCH

HOUSE OF BLUES
CAPITALIZE
I FELCH
Spagos
THE COLLECTOR
OPENS REAL SOON
IRON JOHN
After Dark
STONED LIKE SHIT

The Yearning.
The Passionless Trope.
The Wantan Look.
A Morbid Facination.
A Laceration
Shrimper.
Hi!
I'm Lava!
DON'T BUG ME I BITE!
Unnnh!
I miss the Sun...!
A Hum Job.
A Horney Gaze.
A Rectal Probe.
A Penile Wart.
A Nice Fanny.
It's a doggy-doggy world!
MUSSEL BEACH
Some of my best friends are real dicks!
RED SEA
WATER BOO-Y
SEAL OF APPROVAL
here, here!
MARKY-MARK SPITS
WATER MARK
PUN-ISHED
SEA ENEMY
ALLEY GATOR
Well, I never!
Well, you should have!
PACIFIST OCEAN

Sick!
Grody!
I just think it's sad...
Falling Star
Oh Fuck
That's funny... I don't feel like Vincent Price...
oh, what's the use?
A Weary Sigh.
All right! Who peed in the Pool?
A Trill Shriek.
Minimum Wage.
A Rousing Wrendition.
A Knowing Leer.
An Enigmatic Farce.
Tabula Rasa.
A Tightlip.
Rancour.
A Thickskinned Hart.
A Depressing Sundae.
A Righteous Dude.
I'm pastoral...
I'm floored by my Flora!
We're FLOWERS!
We're growing out of his BUTT!
ALL RIGHT!
Ah-ha!
Some of my best friends are real assholes!
LIQUID PLUMBER
I guess I'm just a Chubby Chaser!
CAT-AMARAN
QUICK CALL 1-800 Jenny
My battery's dead-will you jump me?
I'm Yoko!
ONLY If you'll Swallow...
SPERM WALE
SHAME-ON-YOU THE WHALE
WATER LOG
ANOTHER WATER LOG
WATER HOG
LIQUID NITRATE
WATER BALLOON
WATER-BASED LUBE
HYDRO GIN
I'm the REAL Flipper!
NO KIDDING
LIQUID ASSETS
We got it all together!
MUENSTER
Sea
Ick!

That might have been...
One drink
DRIVER HAS NO CHANGE
NO MORE THAN 3 PICKUPS OR YOU RIDE FREE!
SADISTIC SEX RITUALS OF BALI
UUUURRRP
Too many
Trevor..
Yeah?
RALPH!
How Come everything you do is
so ADORABLE?

Viper Room
Viper Room
I'm Lava!
Viper Room
PAUL LYNDE
CHARLES NELSON RIELLY
HOWARD JOHNSONS
PAT SEJAK
This Week
MARY CHAPIN CARPENTER
PAT BOONE
DONT GIVE ME ANY
HI I'M KURT COBAIN
Thinking about the ways I used to see in
GIANT ERASOR FOR BIG MISTAKES
EMPTY
Thinking about Death
LEFT OUT IN THE RAIN
TNT
ugh!
Where will we live
Where will we live
FATHER RAN AWAY

INSIDE THE VIPER ROOM...
"I saw the worst minds of my generation'... no, 'the biggest airheads of'... no, the best mimes of my...'
WRRRRRRRRRR
RESERVED
NOW I CAN SEE LIKE I USED TO

1. Charo
2. Suzzane Sommers
3. Judd Nelson
4. Trevor Machine
5. Doug
6. Ronny (an aspiring actor)
7. MacCuley Culkin
8. Michael J. Fox
9. Burl Ives
10. Kathy Lee Gifford
11. Mickey Rooney
12. Edward G. Robinson
13. Michael Redgrave
14. River Phoenix
15. Keanu Reeves
16. Madanna
17. Bette Davis
18. Barbara Streisand
19. Frank
20. Montgomery Clift
21. Roody (an aspiring actor)
22. Paul Lynde
23. Carol Channing
24. Juliette Lewis
25. Leonardo de Caprio
26. Thalloolah Bankhead
27. Toody (an aspiring actor)

Maestro.
He's tripping.
Later I'll get him to do a voice-over here describing his hallucinations.
PRODUCT PLACEMENT
mmmmmmmmmmm The Welcome Mat's Out.
(Doug's fingers)
(Trevor's crack)
You're...A...freak
The Welcome mats out. Fu-u-uc-ck.
Totally hairless.

RIVER. RIVER!
AMBULANCE.
AMBULANCE!

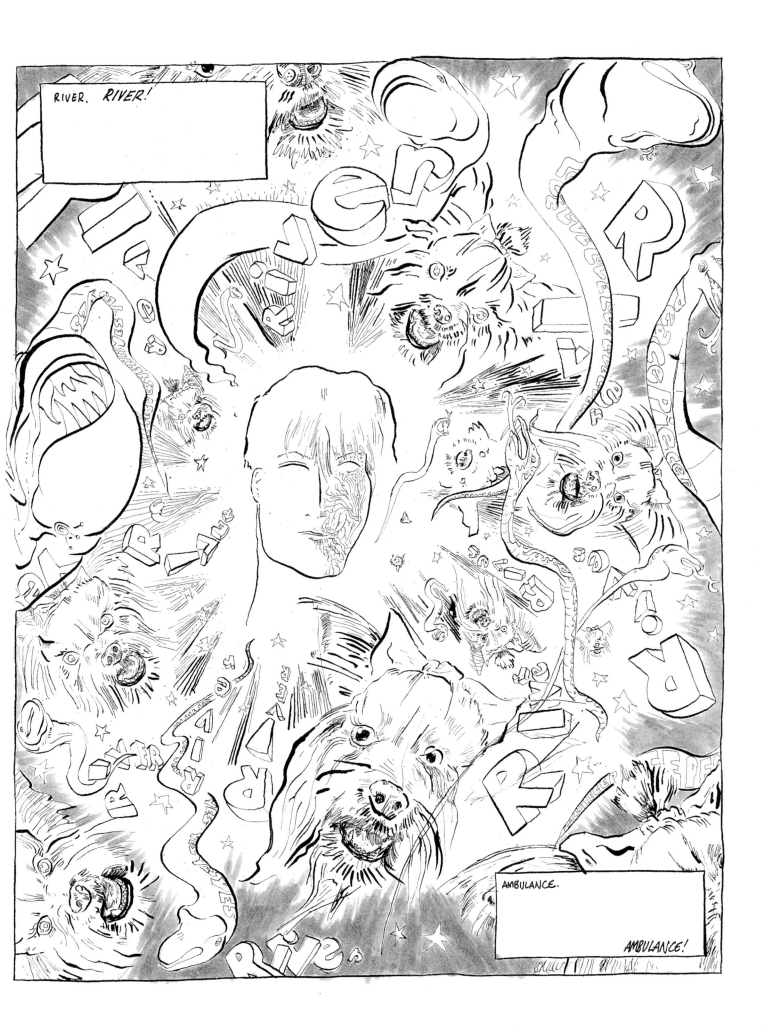

★ RIVER PHOENIX ★
PSSSSSST
BSSSSST
WHO I WAS AND NOW WANT TO DIE.

* RIVER PHOENIX

TREVOR MACHINE

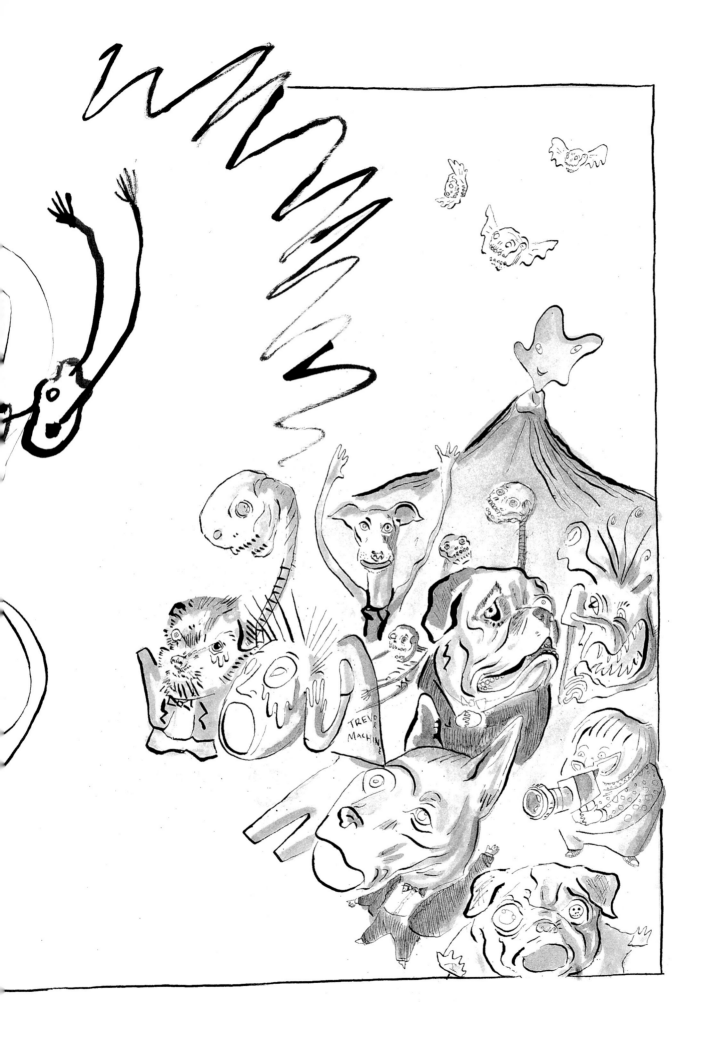

DEVAN
BASS
DULL
GUITAR
INTENSE.
KIMBERLY
DRUMS
I JUST WANT TO BREATHE.
OBJECT FINDER
McDONALDS
BURGER KING
JACK N' THE BOX
WENDY'S
IN N' OUT
WHITE CASTLE
You Okay, Asshole?
DeVan (bass)
DULL GUITAR
Kimberly DRUMS
TREVOR MACHINE
Somebody hand me a pen.
Somebody hand me a pen.
Jesus Christ, Trevor.
DeVan bass
DULL GUITAR
What are you guys doing here?
SCRIBBLE SCRIBBLE
Kimberly (DRUMS)
!
?
You called
DEVAN (bass)
Kimberly
and asked us to meet you here...
SNIFF
Kimberly DRUMS
Hey, what's up?

you don't rem em ber?
RIver Phoenix O.d.ed
right over there. Like...
half an hour ago...
WHAT? I Thought I HALLUCINATED THAT!
Yeah, an ambulance took him away but he was AlReady TOTALLy Fucked.
X-RAY VISION
I KNOW... IT'S LAME OF ME TO... CARE BUT...
SNIFFLE
Oh Shit...
TREVOR MACHINE
WAAA

CRUELLA
EXIT
Shoot this kid's ass...
VIPER ROOM WET BAR
DULL GUITARIST
CRUELLA WHO?
DeVan (WHO PLAYS BASS for HORROR HOSPITAL)
DIVINE MISS M
Johnny Depp
(WALKING UP TO THE GROUP)
We're Closing. You people have to leave.
DULL GUITARIST
TAP TAP TAP

STILL supposed to be JOHNNY DEPP
JOHNNY DEPP!
Get the fuck out of here!
JOHNNY DEPP
What's Leonardo di Caprio Like?
What was it like to work with John Waters?
EXIT
Shoot his ass
to work What was it like
with Tim Burton?
EXIT
Leave this World
Because it's fucked
I don't give a shit
Where I fucking end up
It's all the fucking SAME
When you

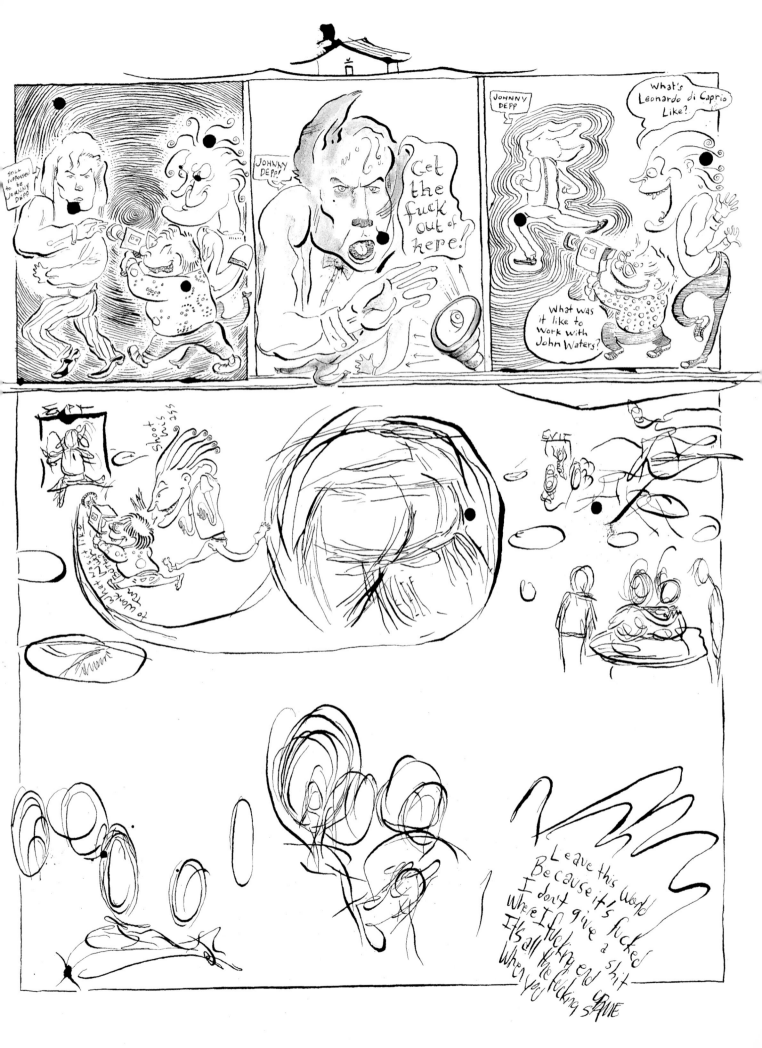

THE NEXT DAY
FIFTH COLUMN
KIMBERLY
BRUCE LEE
DEVAN
FARRAH FAWCETT
BIKINI KILL
QUEER AS F--K
QUEER AS F--K
PEGGY LEE
PAT BENATAR
CLASH
PATTI SMITH
IRON BUTTERFLY
P.J. HARVEY
PUSSY GALORE
Wow, where did you get the naked picture of Lukas Haas?
QUEER AS Fxxk
off the internet. Cool, huh?
So I guess we should start. As the two queer members of Horror Hospital, do you feel your point of view is being adequately represented in the bands music?
Is this real?
ACTUALLY, ANOTHER MEMBER IS... PRETTY SURE HE'S QUEER
YOU DON'T MEAN... THE SINGER?
YEP.
BUT HE HAS A PROBLEM WITH LABELS.
OH MY GOD! YOU MEAN THERE'S A
REMOTE POSS-IBILITY
THAT... I MEAN..
THAT HE'S...
THAT HE'S AVAILABLE
SO I GUESS YOU'RE PRO-OUTING.

WHAT? No, no. See, Trevor's not queer, he's... undecided. He'd tell you that himself if he were here.
Trevor likes to eat shit and get fistfucked.
And he's into big, fat, fifty year old bear types.
Oh.
BOILED ANGEL
DIAM ONDA GALAS
MAL DO ROR
I DON'T CARE BEAR
No he's NOT.
It sounds more like Devan's talking about Himself.
Hm.
Yeah. I could get into that.
QUEER AS FxxK
KARMA SUTRA

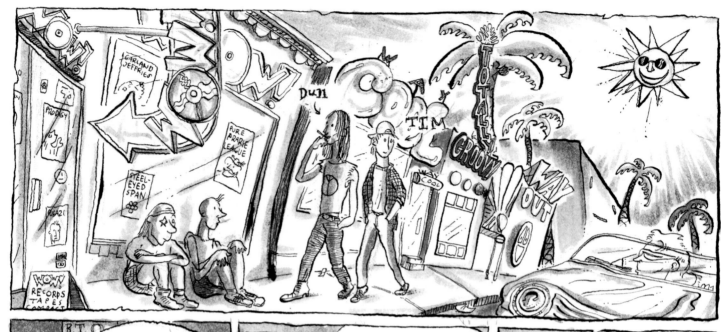

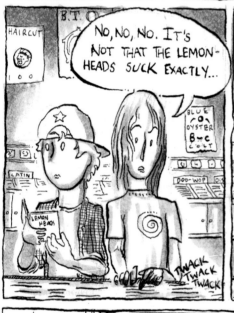

NO, NO, NO. IT'S NOT THAT THE LEMON-HEADS SUCK EXACTLY...

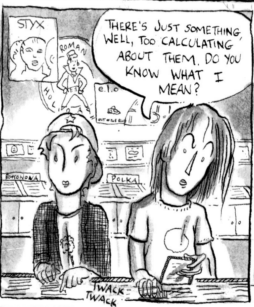

THERE'S JUST SOMETHING WELL, TOO CALCULATING ABOUT THEM. DO YOU KNOW WHAT I MEAN?

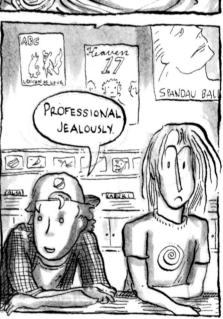

PROFESSIONAL JEALOUSLY.

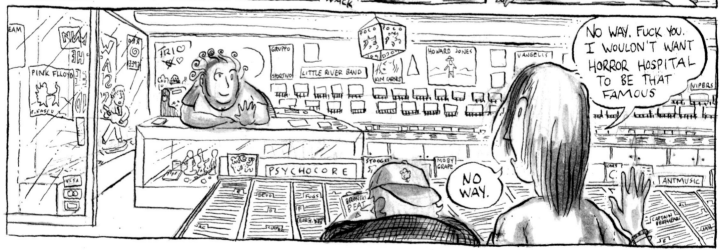

NO WAY. FUCK YOU. I WOULDN'T WANT HORROR HOSPITAL TO BE THAT FAMOUS

NO WAY.

Hey, you're the...
How weird. Another one of you guys was just in here. The singer.
What did he buy?
TALKING HEADS 77
THE JAM
GANG OF FOUR
BLACK FLAG
NO CHECKS PLEASE
MELODY MAKER
um... a Guided By Voices single...
Excellent.
The Shellac album, on vinyl...
Excellent.
and, um...
LIVE AID
TROUSER PRESS
SPECIALS
the new Tori Amos CD.
WHAT?!
Cool!
Shit. Can you hear that?
BOOM BOOM BOOM BOOM BOOM BOOM BOOM BOOM BOOM BOOM BOOM BOOM BOOM BOOM
DAVID BOWIE
T. REX
SWEET
New York Dolls

BOOM
B O O M
The Li'l Cave
B O O M
WOW! WOW! WOW!
FUCKING GAY ASSHOLES.
B O O M
Boom
HEY, WAIT.
TEA DANCE TUESDAY
WEENIE WEDNESDAY
WOW RECORDS TAPES THOSE ROUND THINGS
U2
BEATLES FOR SALE
POOPSI ENTER
She said 'gay' assholes.
not 'queer' assholes.
Oh...
Cool.
B O O M
Boom
Come on, man. One beer.
B O O M
B O O M
Boom
Boom
BEER
Uh, no, no. I have to... Uh, later.

FROGGER
SPLAT!
SPLAT!
SPLAT!

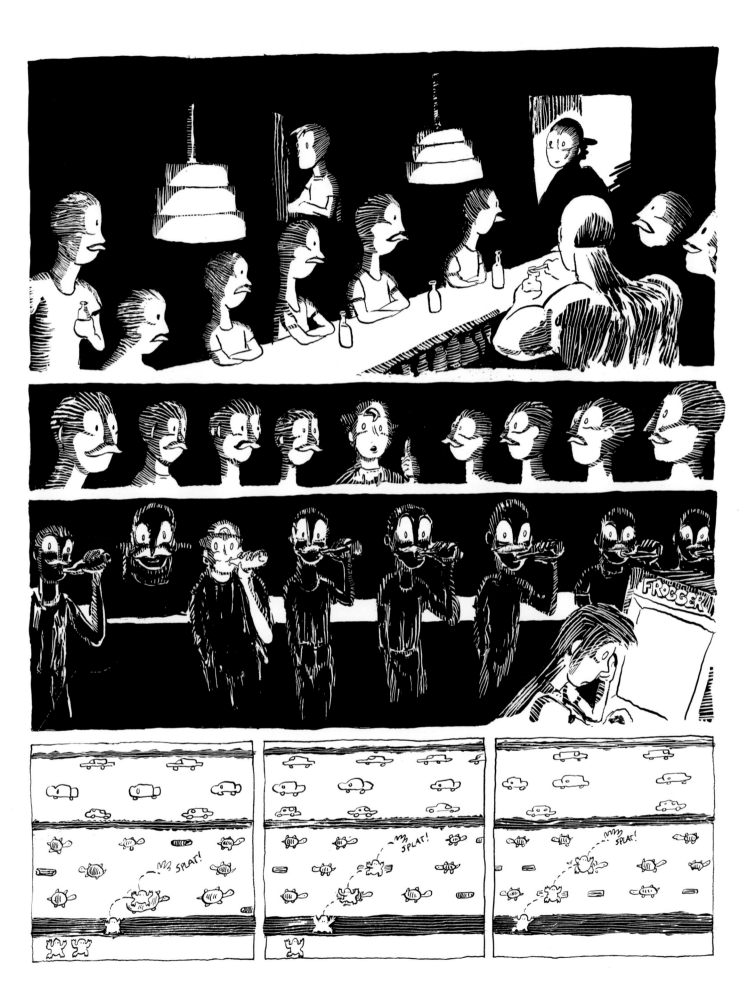

Are you, like, trying to kill those frogs?
MAYBE.
Feel like a challenge match?
No.
PISS, SHIT, FUCK...
FROGGER
BANG
BANG
FROGGER
My name's Tim. And you're...?
FAMOUS.
FROGGER
HEY- DON'T I KNOW YOU?
FROGGER
WINK
OH SHIT.
LOOK, UH, CAN YOU PRETEND YOU'RE MY BOYFRIEND? JUST FOR, LIKE, A SECOND? I'LL PAY YOU BACK.

So, baby, how was, uh... work today?
You're such a beautiful boy...
STROKE!
I'LL TOTALLY FUCKING KILL YOU!
SLAPPITY SLAP SLAP
PUNCH PUNCH PUNCH
PUNCH
PUNCH
FLICK!
FROGG
Oh, son, I'm sorry. I didn't...
IT'S Allright. Just... go away, okay?
Oh shit.
Come on, Trevor. Let's hit the bathroom.

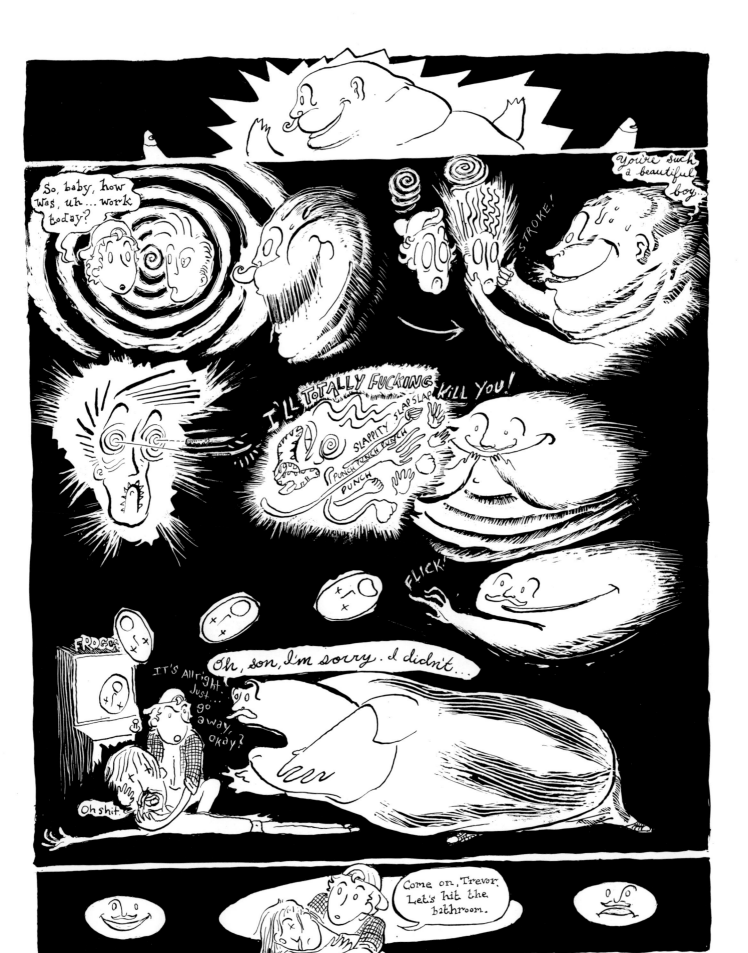

SHIT SHIT SHIT...
Look, uh, lie on the floor. That should stop the blood flow. I'll guard the door.
WHERE DO I KNOW YOU FROM?
Through Dull.

Give us a second, okay?
I've met you a couple of times.
OH, RIGHT.
HI.
Hi.

When the blood stops, we can go to my place, if you want, and get you cleaned up. If that's okay and everything. I've got a washing machine and all that sort of stuff.
18. How old are you?
OKAY, BUT... HOW OLD ARE YOU?
I don't know. Why do you care?
18. WHY DO YOU FUCKING CARE?
AWESOME.

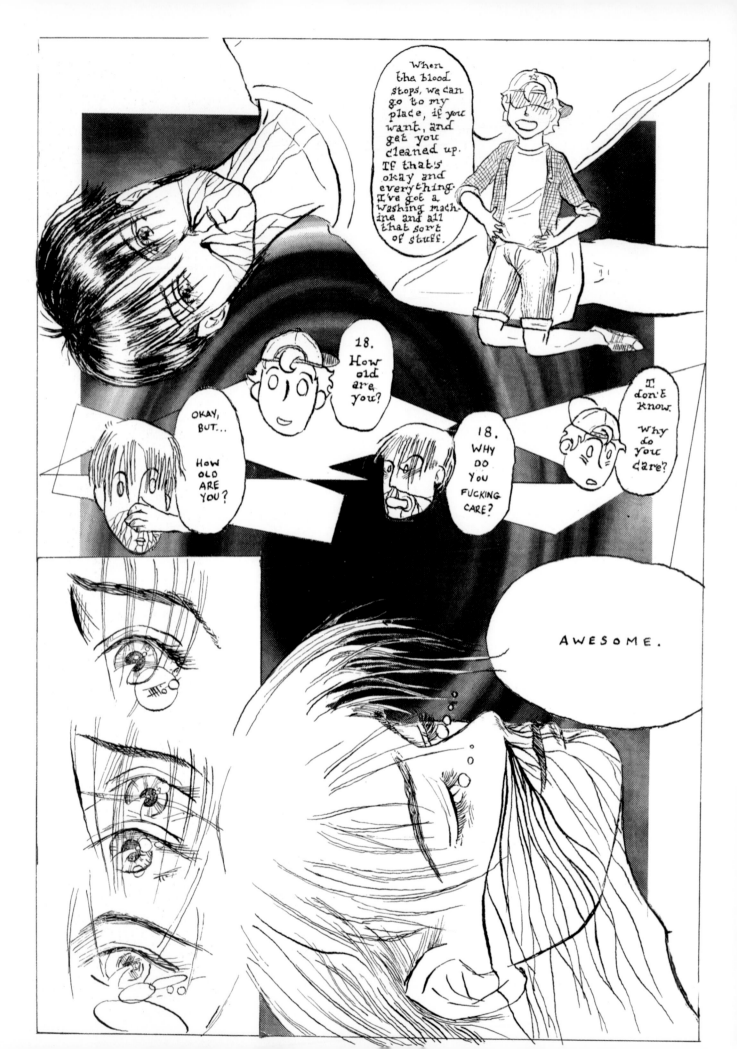

THE 120 MINUTES ᵒᶠ SODOM

3 WEEKS LATER
So... WHY DO YOU ALWAYS WANT TO, UH... LICK ME AND STUFF?
'Cos nobody loves me / It's true / Not like you do
Because you're beautiful.
IF YOU'RE DYING...
ADVOCATE
exclusive
I'M NOT GAY, BUT I KNOW PEOPLE WHO ARE
SLIP N SLIDE
PORTISHEAD
DUMMY

YEAH, I KNOW, BUT... I DON'T UNDERSTAND WHAT YOU GET OUT OF IT. I MEAN... IT'S JUST MY DICK.
roll over.
OH FUCK.
OKAY, BUT... IT KIND OF WEIRDS ME OUT WHEN YOU DO THIS.
enjoy.
I AM, I GUESS. I MEAN, I HAVE THE BONER FROM HELL.
ADVOCATE
BEING QUEER IS SO WEIRD.

I THOUGHT IT WOULD BE WEIRDER THAN THIS.
I LIKE IT, BUT...

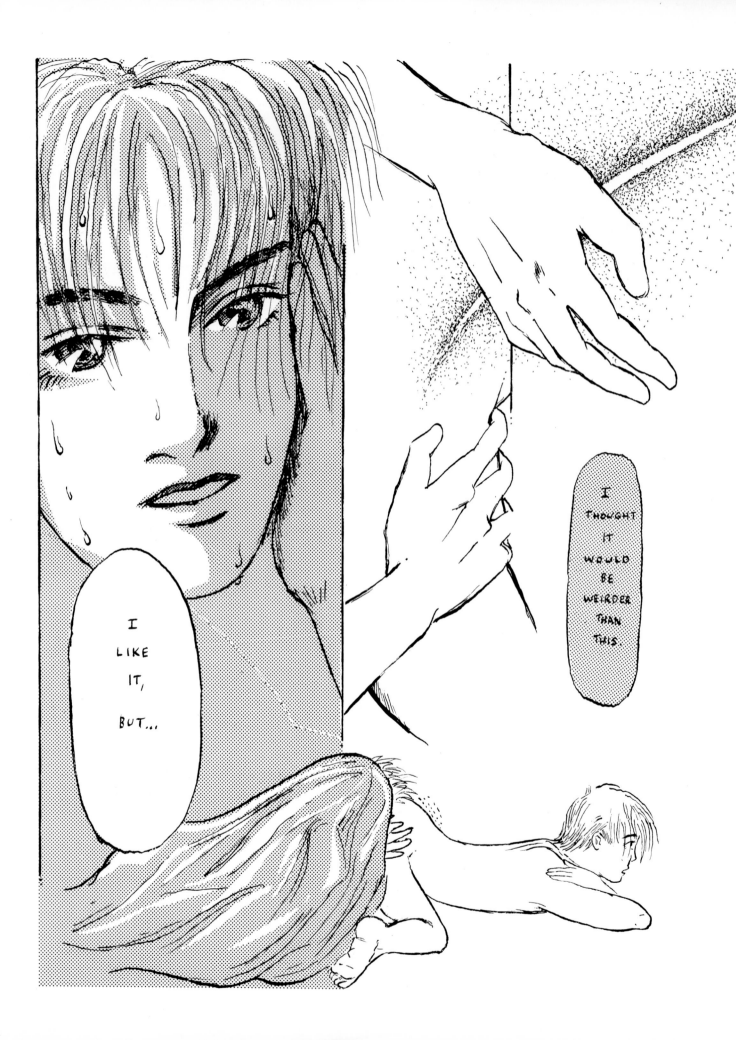

OR NOT WEIRDER, BUT...
THAT I'D JUST DO IT ONCE IN A WHILE
LIKE I DO ACID
BUT I WOULDN'T
YOU KNOW
UH...
LOOK TIM, UH MAYBE YOU SHOULDN'T...
I MEAN, I HAD MEXICAN FOOD FOR DINNER
AND, UH...
Your ass is so perfect.

UH THANKS...
I THINK.
BUT, UH, YOU SHOULD PROBABLY STOP WHAT YOU'RE DOING
RIGHT THIS SECOND.
IF YOU CATCH MY DRIFT.
If I gave you a ring would you wear it?
OH, YECCCH. YOUR BREATH SMELLS LIKE MY BUTT.
WAIT.
IT SMELLS KIND OF COOL!

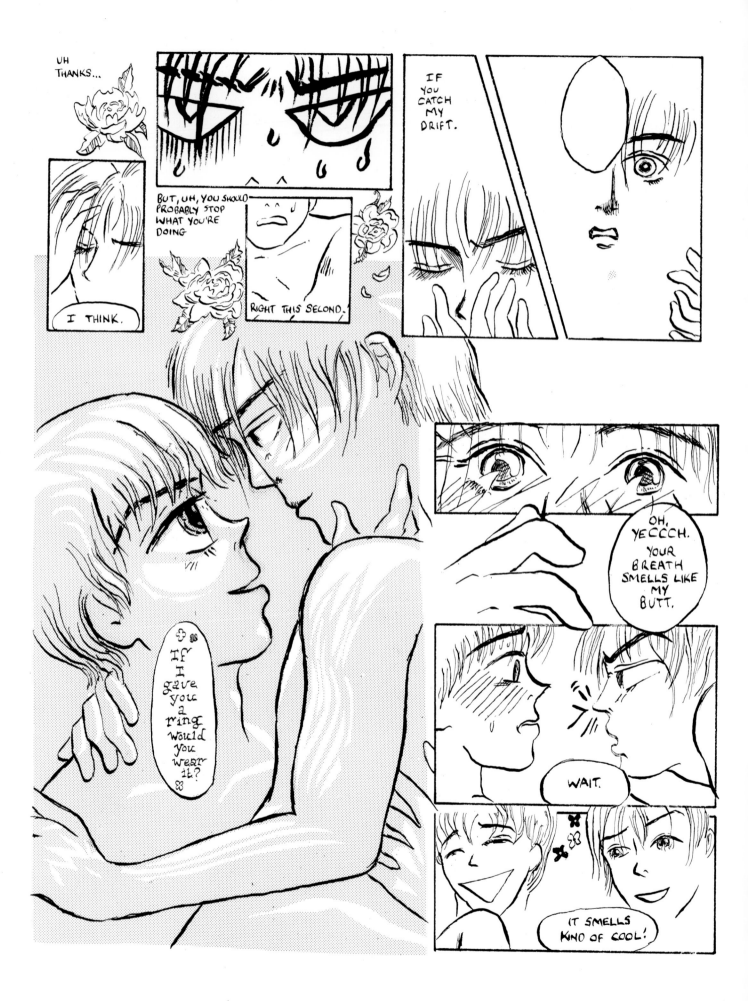

I love you Trevor.
OH YEAH?
and you love me. you can't say so, but I know you do.
NO I DON'T.
LOVE IS, UH...
A LIE.

Give it up, Trevor. You're the sweetest guy in the world, like it or not.
NO I'M NOT.
YOU JUST SEE ME WHEN I'M IN A GOOD MOOD.
MOST OF THE TIME I'M REALLY FUCKED UP.
IT'S LIKE... YOU KNOW WHO TRENT REZNOR IS, RIGHT?
EVIL.
DANGEROUS.

DID YOU READ THAT INTERVIEW WITH HIM IN DETAILS?
WELL, HE TALKED ABOUT THAT.
HOW SOMETIMES HE'S A REALLY NICE, NORMAL GUY. BUT THEN HE'LL GET JUST...
POSSESSED
Why don't you write a song about what you're feeling right now.

I dare you...
I COULD IF I FUCKING FELT LIKE IT!
OKAY, FINE, ASSHOLE.
YOU GOT A PEN?
CAN I WRITE ON THIS PILLOW?
Sure.
WELL, HERE'S A MARX-A-LOT.

MAYBE YOU SHOULD HUG ME OR SOMETHING WHILE I'M WRITING, IF YOU FEEL LIKE IT...
BECAUSE IT MIGHT, UH
INSPIRE ME
Love's a lie
and I hope
but I'm not a liar

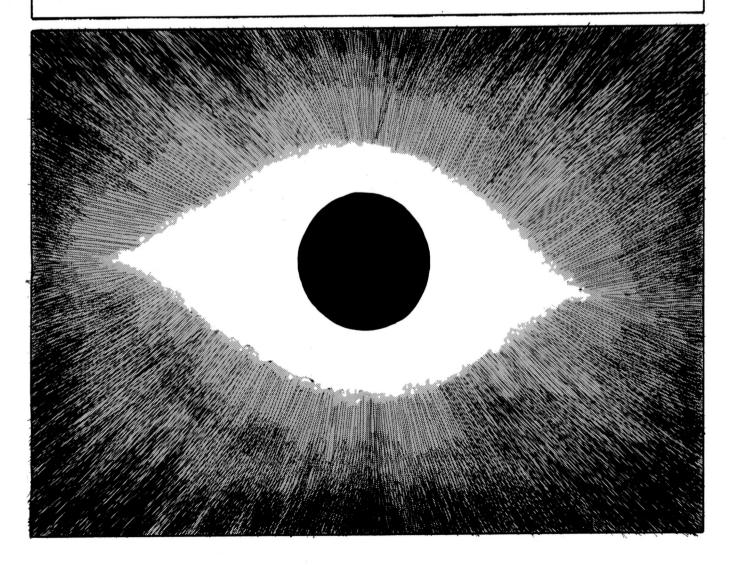

CLICK
OKAY, WE'RE SET IN HERE. LET US KNOW WHEN YOUR VOCALIST ARRIVES.
SHIT!
WHERE IS HE?
Getting porked by that CLONE.
HEY, TIM'S OKAY.
HE'S JUST A LITTLE CONVENTIONAL.
KIMBERLY (DRUMS)
DEVAN (BASS)
DULL (GUITAR)
XXX

What do you think they do in bed? It's got to be really boring, right? I bet they just look into each others eyes and shoot their loads without even having to touch them-selves
and grot-esque shit like that.
TREVOR'S LIFESTYLE IS HIS BUSINESS. I JUST WISH IT WASN'T WASTING US $300 AN HOUR OF STUDIO TIME.
But his lyrics have turned to shit. Dull. Those last two songs could've been written by Elton John!
I still can't believe Trevor's involved with someone.
Not that I have anything against relationships.
It's just...
I THOUGHT TREVOR WAS BEYOND STUFF LIKE LOVE AND SEX.

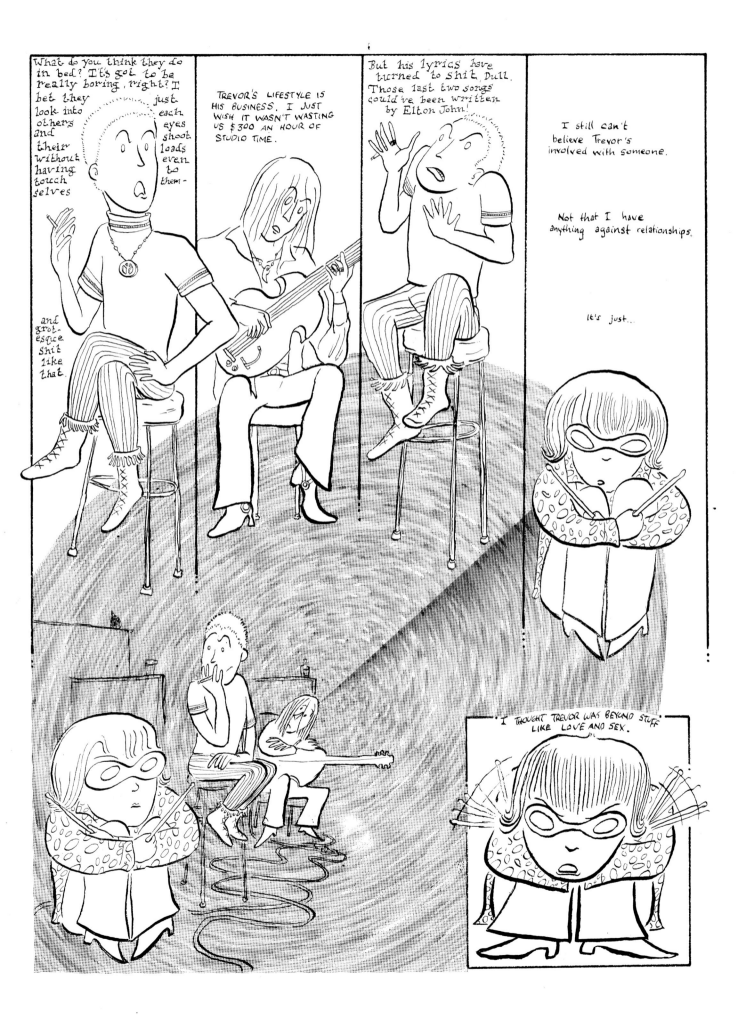

CREEEK!
!
!
!
COURTNEY LOVE!
am I supposed to be here?

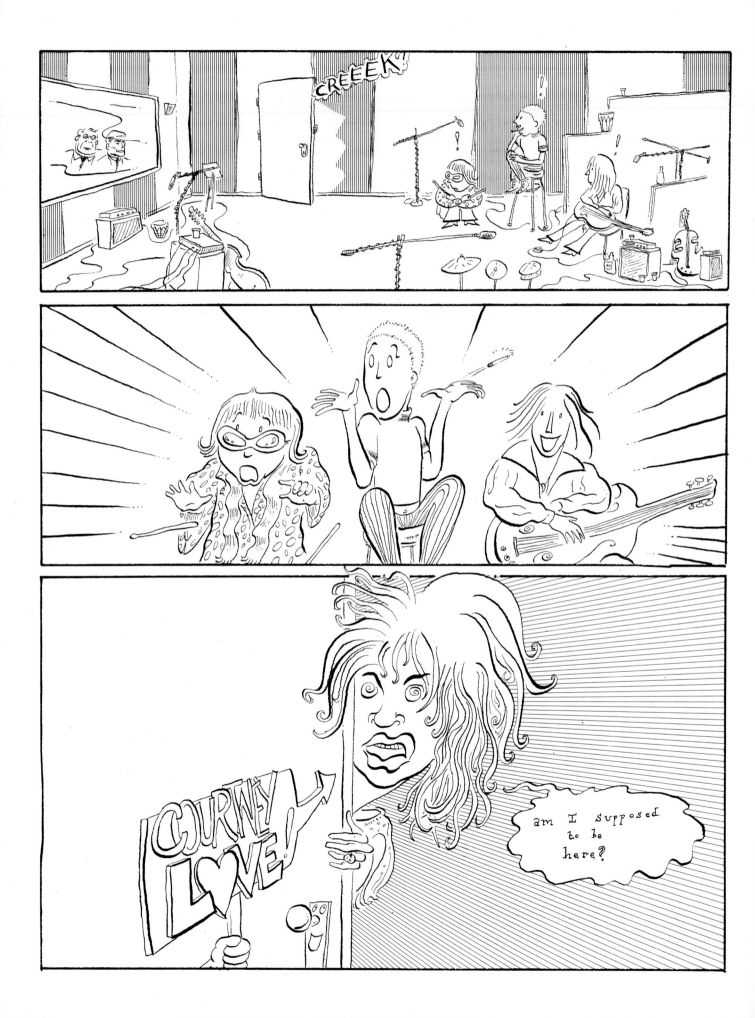

UH, NO...
I mean
YEAH! MAYBE YOU ARE!
great.
finally.
What a shithole. It reminds me of the Punk Rock Days. Going to bed with some speed freak skateboard fucking neanderthal. Waking up with a vomit facial.
What am I supposed to be doing here anyway? I forget.

UH... sing a song with us? You know, as a guest vocalist?
I don't rember setting this up.
YEAH, YOU REMEMBER! WE'RE, LIKE... KURT SORT OF, UH, WAS GOING TO PRODUCE OUR ALBUM, BUT, YOU KNOW, HE, UH... DID WHAT HE DID INSTEAD, AND, UH, YOU SAID YOU'D MAKE IT UP TO US BY SINGING ON OUR DEMO!
Oh yeah! Kurt loved you guys! You were the only band he really respected. Well, you and R.E.M. So what do you want me to sing?
FLING!
TREVOR MACHINE
THE FABER BOOK OF GAY SHORT FICTION
CHEST O' SONGS
HORROR HOSPITAL

Sorry I'm Late!
HOW?
SHAME!
WOW
AAOOGAH
100% KOSHER
OH MY GOD! WHAT A BEAUTIFUL LITTLE BOY! DO YOU HAVE A GIRLFRIEND?
He's a fag.
WHATEVER.

HERE, SING THIS ONE. YOU AND TREVOR CAN DO A DUET.
(IT'S THE RIVER PHOENIX MEMORIAL SONG. PERFECT OR WHAT?)
SNAP!
WE'RE RICH.

THE WORLD
IS A VIPER ROOM!
NO SAINTS ALLOWED
HEY RIVER!
YOU DIED!
BUT YOU FLOWED SO HARD!

ONE WEEK LATER AT GEFFEN RECORDS...

BUT YOU

HOSPITAL
HORROR
IRVANA
EVERMIND"

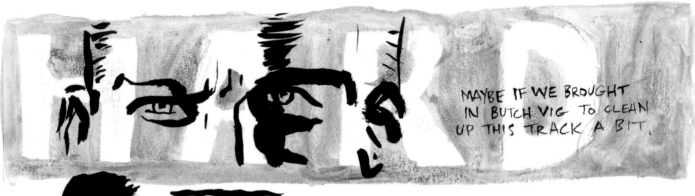

MAYBE IF WE BROUGHT
IN BUTCH VIG TO CLEAN
UP THIS TRACK A BIT.

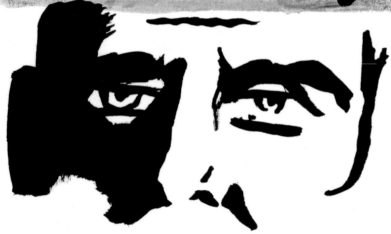

AND SPIKE JONZE
TO DO THE VIDEO.

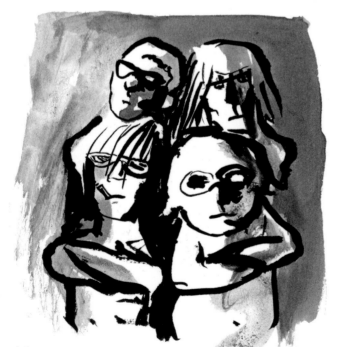

HORROR HOSPITAL

CUTE.

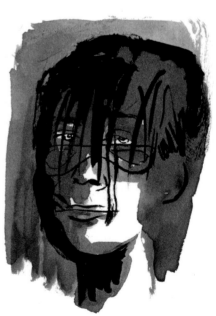

TREVOR

VERY
CUTE IN ONE
CASE.

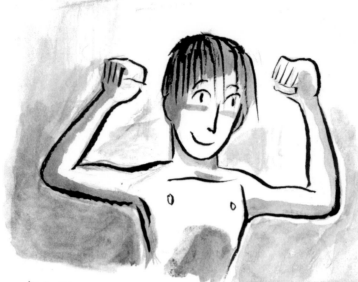

DAVID WILL LOSE HIS MIND OVER THIS KID.

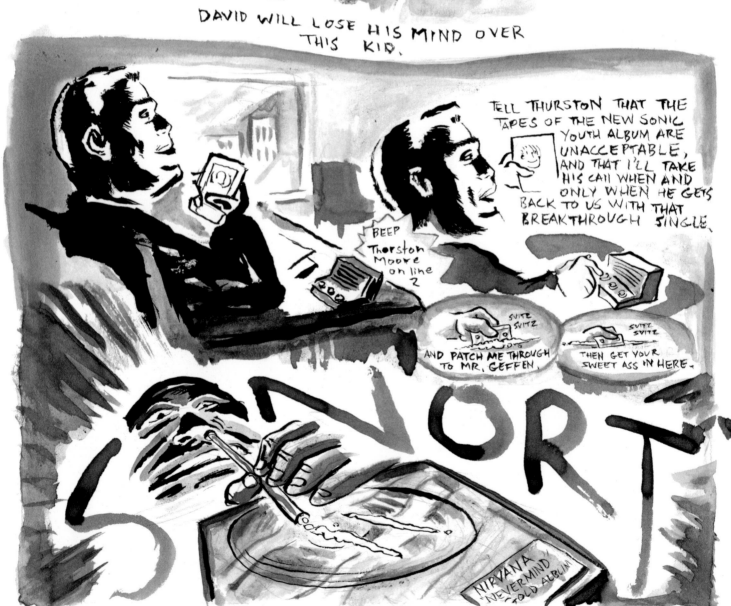

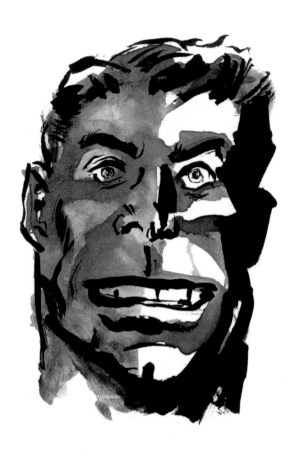

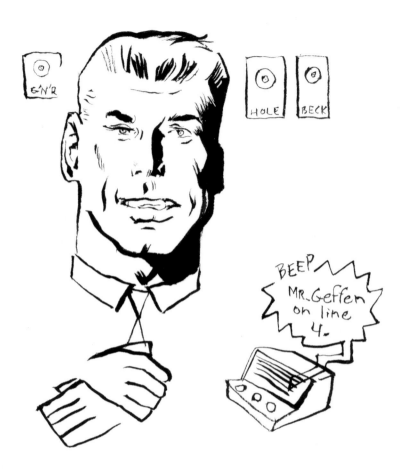

G'N'R

HOLE   BECK

BEEP
MR. Geffen
on line
4.

DAVID. I THINK I'VE
COME ACROSS SOMETHING
YOU'LL FIND INTER-
ESTING. A BAND
CALLED

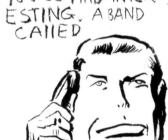

HORROR HOSPITAL.

ALSO
I THINK
YOU
MIGHT
WANT
TO TAKE
A LOOK
AT THEIR
SINGER

HE'S
VERY
"YOU".

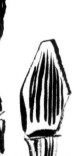

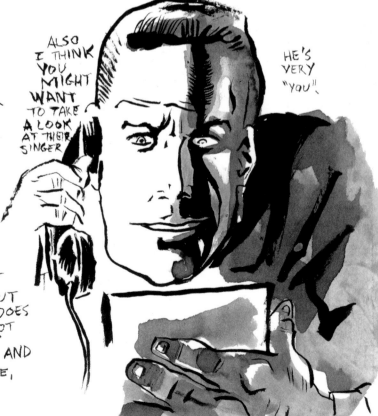

THEY'RE NOVELTY PUNK ROCK, BUT
THERE'S ONE TRACK ON THE DEMO ABOUT
RIVER PHOENIX, AND COURTNEY LOVE DOES
CO-LEAD VOCALS. NEED I SAY WE'VE GOT
A POSSIBLE COLLEGE RADIO SMASH HERE?
BUT IF WE SIGN THEM, IT SHOULD BE IN AND
OUT FAST. WE'RE TALKING A KING MISSILE,
DREAD ZEPPELIN, CRASH TEST DUMMIES
TYPE OF THING.

BUFFY SAINTE-MARIE
SAVOY BROWN
SILVER CONVENTION
SPARKS
LOCAL ACT?
SLAUGHTER
SAM & DAVE
LEO SAYER
SLADE
STARLAND VOCAL BAND
SEEDS
PHOEBE SNOW
STREISAND
SNAIL
SUBDUDES
APPARENTLY.
CHECK OUT THEIR LIVE SHOW
NEVERMIND

and have an intern run their photo up to me
RIGHT
GOD I love GAY MEN
CLICK
THEY'RE SO PREDICTABLE.

MEANWHILE, ACROSS TOWN:

SUN-NO
CLOSER
THE WELL OF LONLINESS

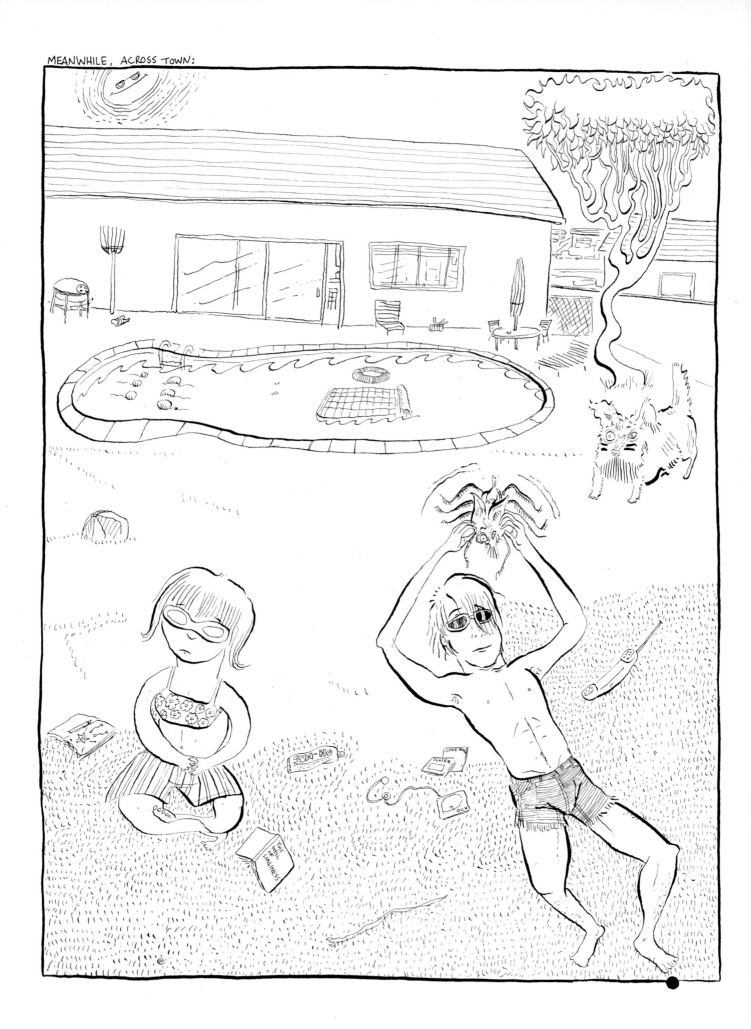

(TEARING OFF THE LEG OF THE COCKROACH)
TOK!
I LOVE HIM
TOOK!
I LOVE HIM NOT
TEEK!
I LOVE HIM!
GO FUCK YOURSEL
You're freaking everyone out, Trevor.
WHAT DO YOU MEAN?
TWEEK!
I LOVE HIM NOT...
(1)
(2)
WAIT!
I LOVE HIM
I LOVE HIM NOT?
FUCK THIS!

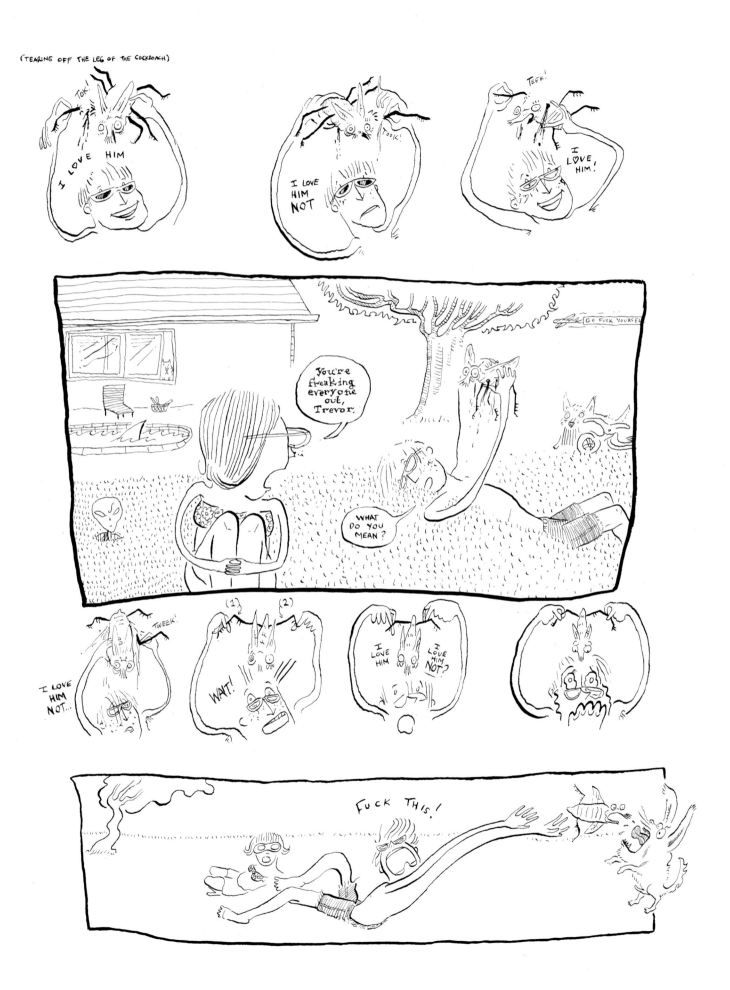

It's cool you're happy and everything. It's just that your lyrics are getting are getting kind of... too nice, you know? I don't mind so much, but Devan's talking about quiting the band!
YEAH, WELL, HE'S A PROMISCUOUS SLEAZEBAG. DID YOU KNOW HE'S SLEEPING WITH THAT CREEPY GUY DOUG? I MEAN DOUG PRACTICALLY RAPED ME!
BRRING!
Trevor Machine former Punk Rock God, at your service...
I'm kidding
HELLO, TREVOR. THIS IS DAVID GEFFEN.

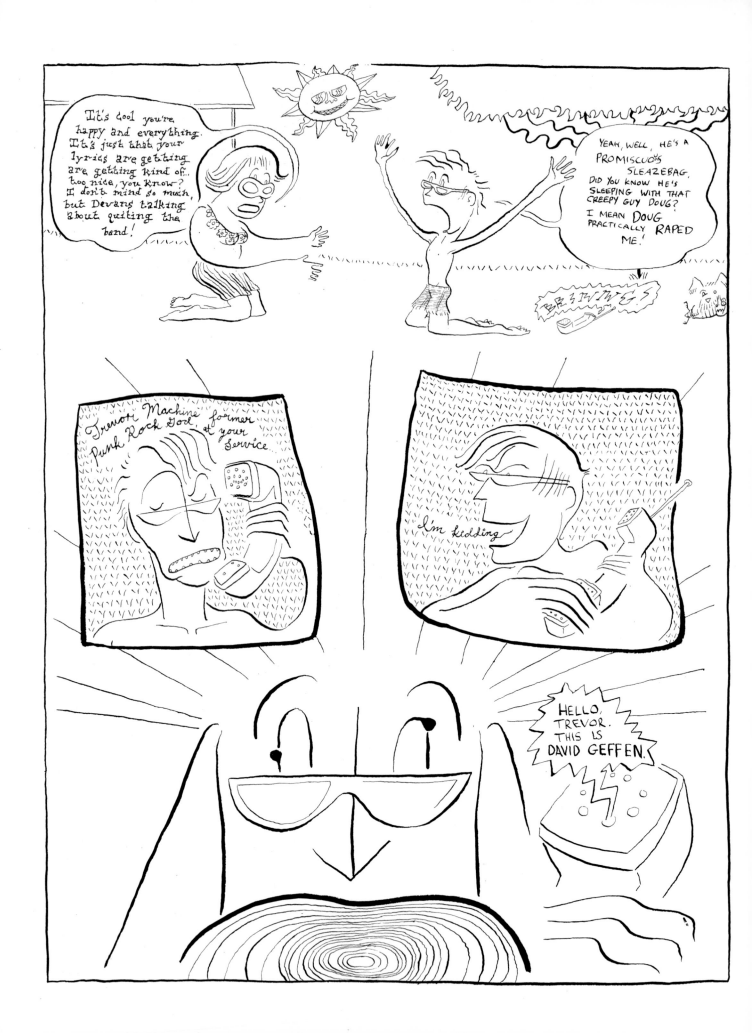

DEVAN! YOU'RE FUCKING EVIL!
Ha, ha. No. It really is DAVID GEFFEN.
I listened to your Demo, and I'm very Impressed.
PROVE IT.
IT'S SOME GUY SAYING HE'S DAVID GEFFEN.
Ask him if he really got married to Keanu Reeves?
No wait! Ask him if Tom Cruise is Gay or not!
I'd like to invite you and your fellow bandmembers to a party at my house tonight. A lot of interesting people will be there. And I know Courtney would like to see you again
OH SHIT. IT'S REALLY YOU. UH... OKAY. COOL. HEY, OUR DRUMMER WANTS TO KNOW IF TOM CRUISE IS GAY OR NOT.
Well she can ask him herself. He'll be there tonight.

Would you like me to give you directions?
SHOOT.
BYE.
WHAT?!

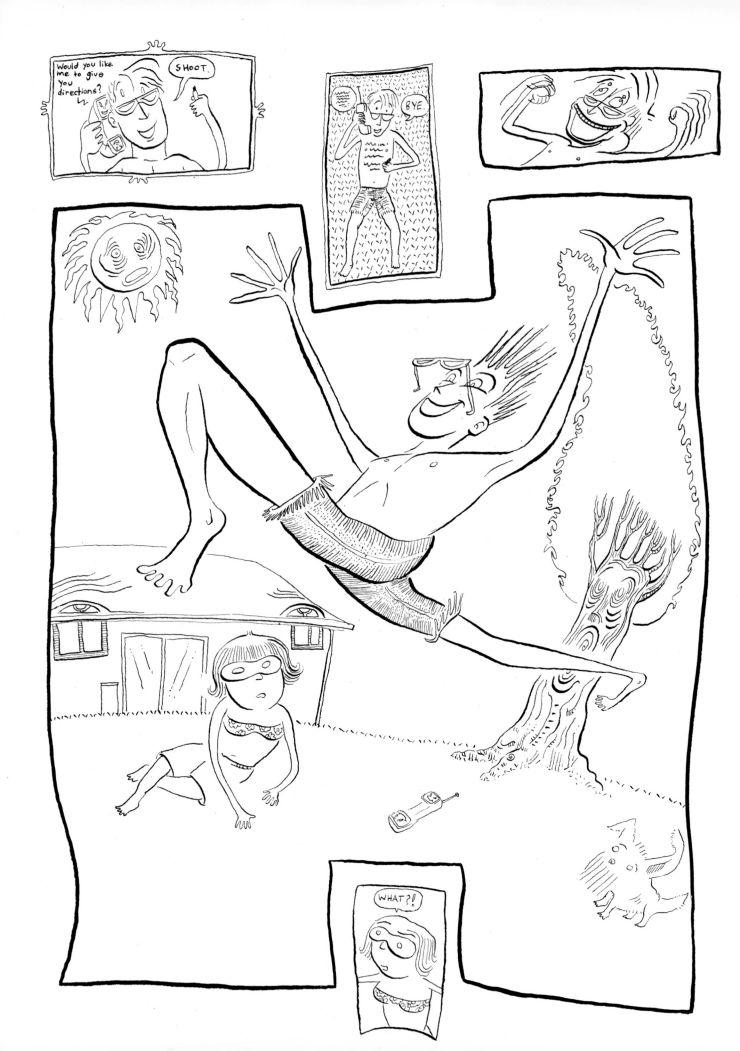

OPEN 24 HOURS
David GEFFEN'S
PRIME RIB DINNER $2.98 · KENO
LOOSE SLOTS
DIESAL
WALMAR
1-800 FUCK ME
That Night
AT DAVID GEFFEN'S Mansion
THIS WAY TO D. GEFFEN 37.2 MILES
GO BACK
RIGHT NOW
THIS MEANS YOU!

Dull
Devan
Kimberly
Trevor
Tim.

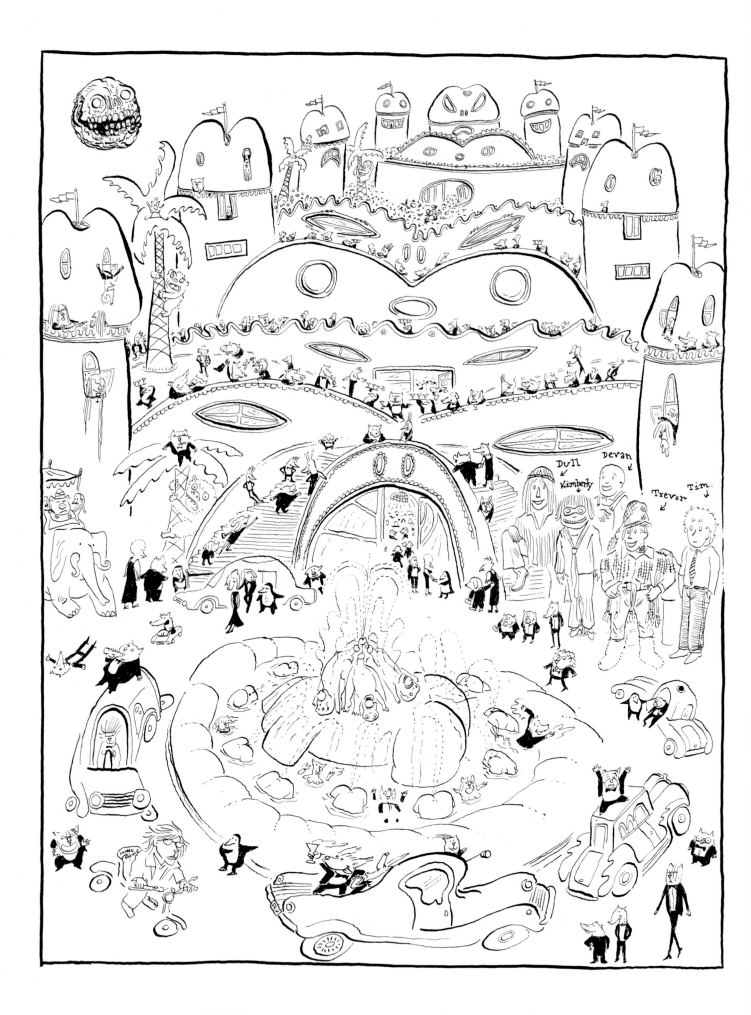

WHICH ONE IS GEFFEN?
This is weird
IT'S TOTALLY PSYCHOTIC...

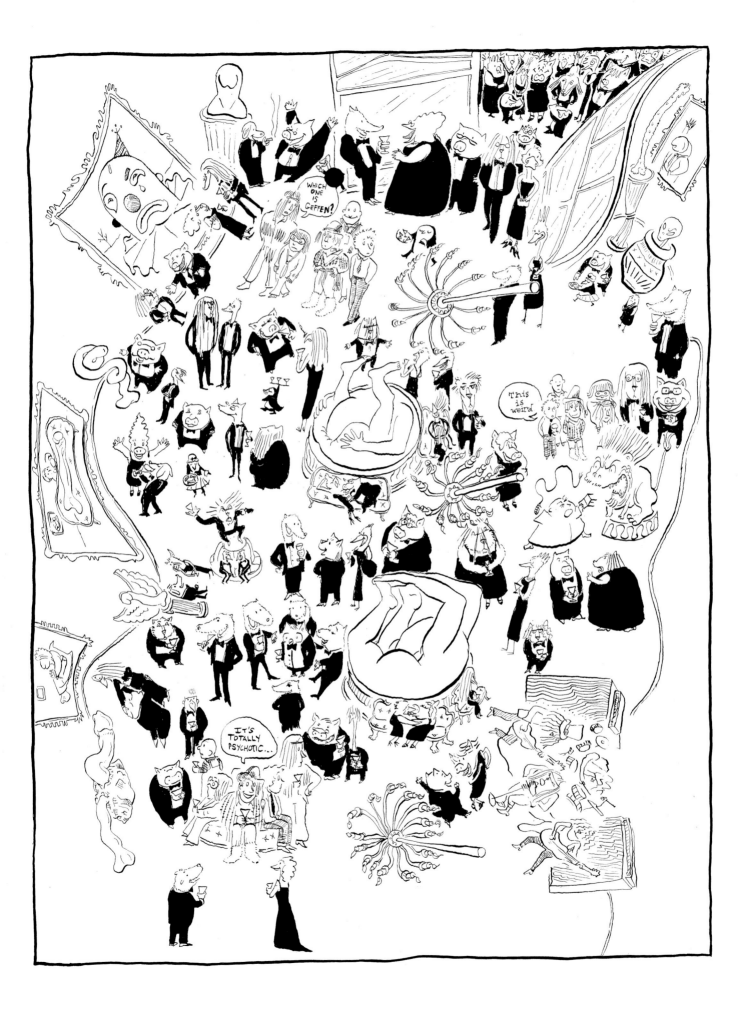

HI I'M LANCE KERWIN
HI I'M CARROL O'CONNOR
HI I'M SOME SOCIETY SHIT
HI I'M SOME BUSINESS TURD
...but it's really cool.
HI I'M ROSANNE
HI I'M SONY CEO
HI I'M HASBEEN DUTCH MODEL
HI, I'M MICHAEL STIPE
HI I'M MARLON BRANDO
I'm going off to shmooze.
See ya.
HI I'M HENRY ROLLINS
HI I'M PAUL LYNDE
WAIT!
I'm going to check out the backyard and smoke a joint. Anybody want to come?
Yeah, actually. I think I need to be a little stoned to get through this.
HI I'M CHARLES NELSON RIELLY
What about you?
I'M COOL. SEE YOU, UH, LATER.

HI I'M PATTI SMITH
HI I'M MARY ANN FAITHFULL
HI I'M ROBERT SMITH
BECK
elastica
are you a friend of David's.
HE WORSHIPS ME.
HI I'M MARK BOLAN
HI I'M BRYAN FERRY
HI I'M TINY TIM
HI I'M SABU
HI I'M HAJI
HI I'M ROONEY ALLEN RIPLEY
I'm not surprised. I'm Ralph, he's Brian. We work in promotion at Geffen Records.
WHERE IS DAVID ANYWAY?
HI I'M RALPH
elastica
HI I'M BRIAN
HI I'M HERVE VILLECHAIZE
HI I'M BILLY BARTY
HI I'M GARY COLEMAN
I just saw him upstairs...
Shall we take you to him?
I'M SURE HE'LL REWARD YOU HANDSOMELY FOR YOUR KINDNESS.
HI I'M RALPH

TIM, OH SHIT! I'M GOING TO MEET FUCKING DAVID GEFFEN!
HI I'M LEO DICAPRIO
HI I'M EDDIE FURLONG
HI I'M MICK JAG
HI I'M JIMI HEN
HI I'M RAINER WERNER FASSBINDER
HI I'M MARCUS SHEKENBERG
HI I'M DAVID BOWIE
HI I'M SID
HI I'M MATT DYLAN
HI I'M CATHERINE DENEUVE
BJORK

HI I'M CHRIS ATKINS
HI WE'RE NELSON
HI I'M DOUG HENNING
HI I'M RAYMOND BURR
HI I'M SIEGFRIED
HI I'M ROY
BULLSHIT! YOU'RE GAY. EVERYBODY KNOWS IT. MY FUCKING MOM KNOWS IT.
Well, I'm not.
HI I'M TOM CRUISE
HI I'M LEO DICAPPRIO
HELLO MY NAME IS SKANK ROYALE

YOU'RE TOTALLY GAY.
COME ON, I CAN TELL JUST FROM LOOKING AT YOU.
ARE YOU TELLING ME THAT IF, UH... I DON'T KNOW... IF LEONARDO DiCAPRIO ASKED YOU TO SLEEP WITH HIM, YOU WOULDN'T BE LIKE, 'WHOA, SCORE!'?
Leonardo's not my... I mean, no, of course not.
JOHN TRAVOLTA!
HI I'M JOHN TRAVOLTA
HI I'M BURT REYNOLDS

HI I'M ROB LOWE
Tom Cruise. How are you doing? Got a sec?
HI I'M. STILL (SUPPOSED TO BE) JOHN TRAVOLTA
AND I'M STILL TOM CROOZE
PATRIC SWAY
Nice talking to you. Here call this number. It might help you find the inner piece you so desperately need.
THE CHURCH OF SCIENTOLOGY HOT LINE?
BRAINWASHED CLOSET QUEEN!

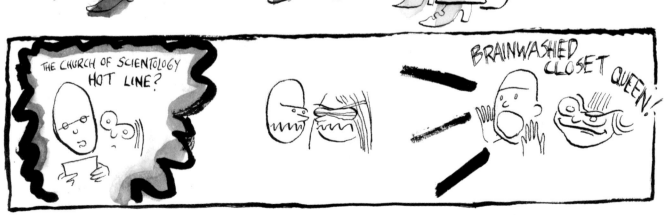

Tim.
Dull.
Courtney
YOU FUCKING RIPPED ME OFF!
HI I'M COURTNEY LOVE
WHAT THE?
COURTNEY, SWEETIE, WHAT SEEMS TO BE THE PROBLEM?

THESE FUCKERS BULLSHITED ME, DAVID. THEY TOLD ME THEY WERE WEEZER SO I'D SING ON THEIR PIECE OF SHIT RECORD.
HI I'M DAVID GEFFEN
No we didn't, Mr. Geffen. Really. I mean, Courtney's a genius and everything, but she's lying.
YOU'RE in Horror Hospital aren't you? Well, I'm glad you could make it. Where's Trevor?

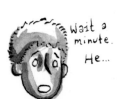 Wait a minute. He...

 I

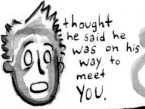 thought he said he was on his way to meet YOU.

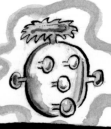

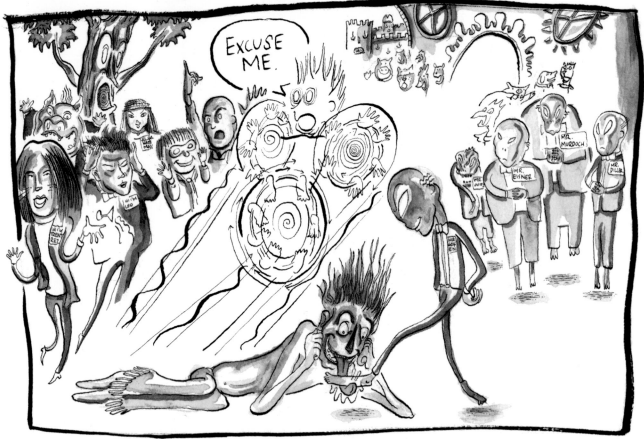 SHIT!

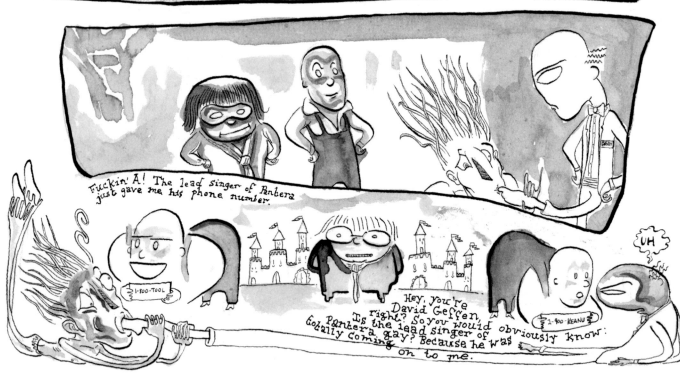

TREVOR?
OH SHIT SHI-I-I-T
TREVOR?
TREVOR?
TREVOR
It's time to take a dive
TREVOR?
TREVOR?

Trevor.
Ralph.
Brian.
LOOK You guys are really NICE and this is sort of INTERESTING but
I'm in a relationship
Hey be careful those are my balls
RELAX I WON'T BITE EM

Are you sure condoms can't break cos
OUCH
TAKE IT EASY BACK THERE!
uh...are you sure-ISNT THAT uh uncool? oh shit what the fuck
GET READY
come in my mouth okay?
TH AR SHE BLOWS

TREVOR?
SHIT

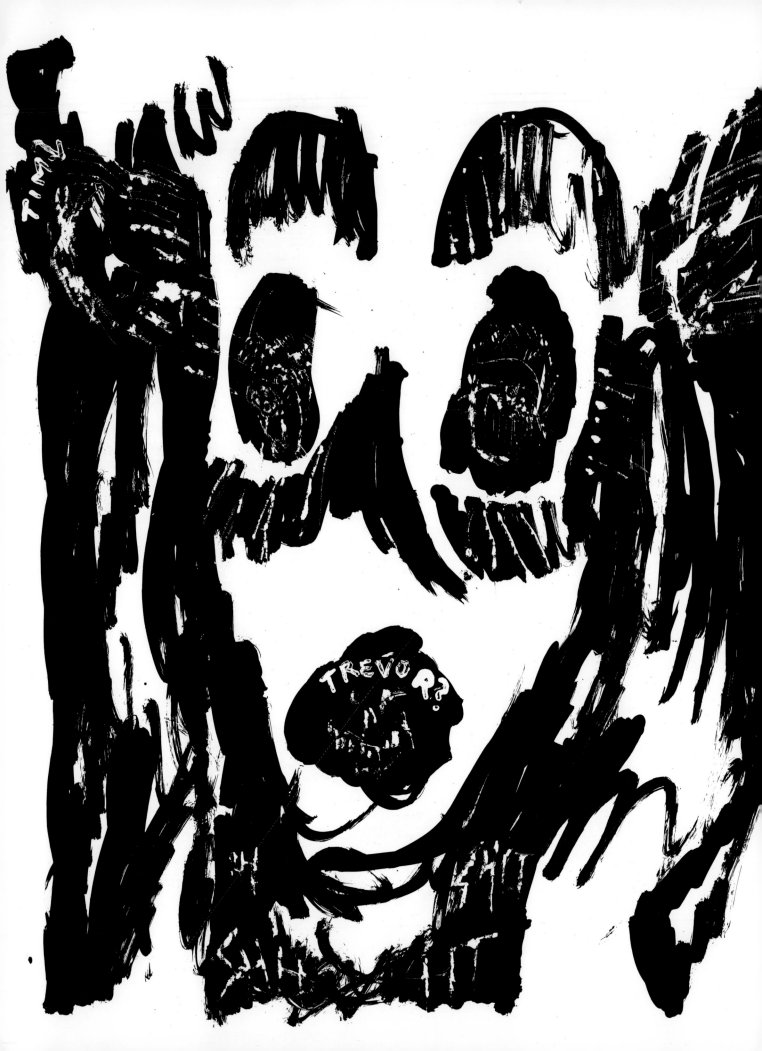

TREVOR YOu're an ASSHOLE
Tim

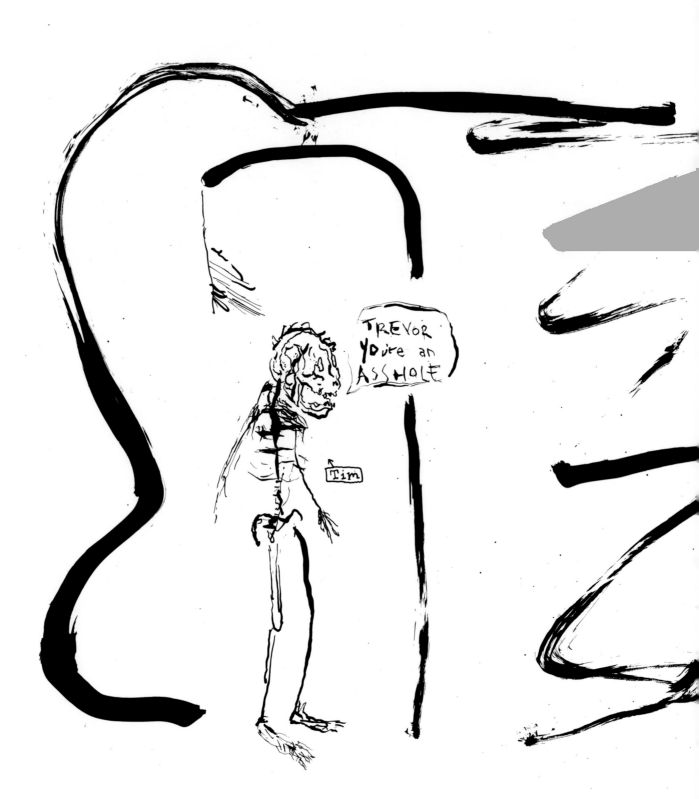

WHAT THE
Kill the lights get the fuck out of here
Trevor
RALPH
BRIAN

OH YEAH YE-AH-AH-AH
CAN H COME IN YOUR MOUTH?
uh... I should probably... uh.... go.
SLAM

L'APPARITION
ACTUALLY, WE JOE COOLS ARE SCARED TO DEATH OF
FARRAH

BRUCE
SPEAKING
with Trevor Machine lead singer, lyricist, and artistic force behind Horror Hospital. Mr. Machine, where do you get the inspiration for your darkly poetic lyrics?
OK, DOUG, GO FOR IT.

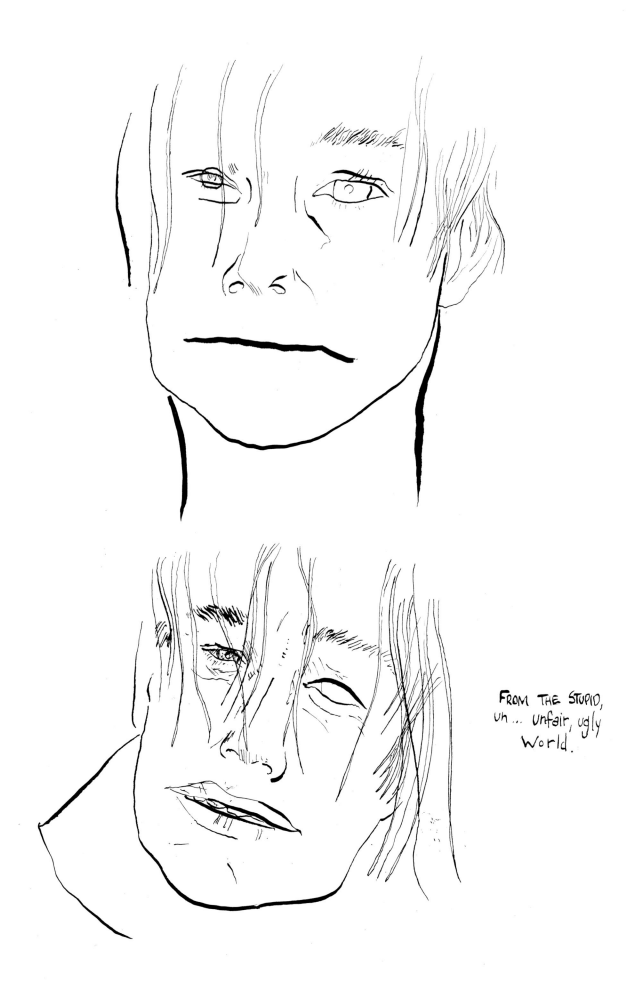

FROM THE STUPID,
uh ... unfair, ugly
World.

ROXY MUSIC
Could you name some of the bands that have influenced you?
NONE. I HATE MUSIC. I DON'T LISTEN TO IT.
oh really?
Let's move on, shall we?

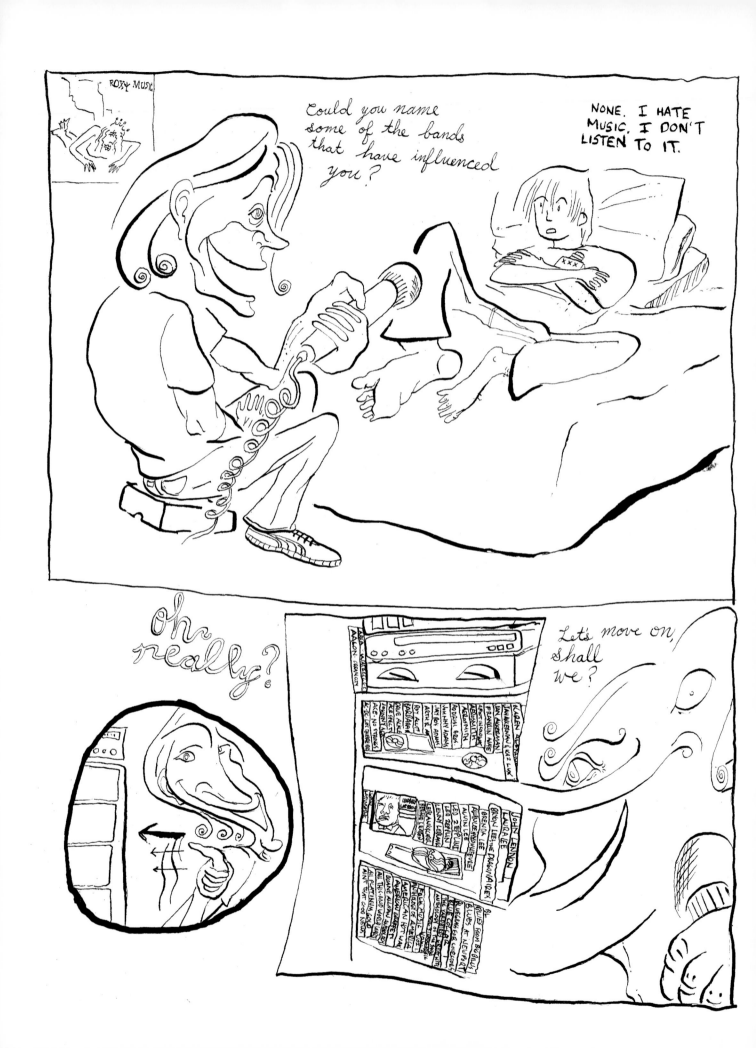

Do you think your music is influenced by your homosexuality
XXX
I'M NOT GAY.
XXX
okay, maybe I was sort of gay for about a week, but...

LOVE AND SEX ARE A LIE!
AND I'M SAYING THAT AS SOMEONE WHO'S BEEN THERE AND GOT TOTALLY BURNED!
Those songs about love are
the worst shit I ever wrote and we'll never play them again n
no matter how much the audience begs us.

TAKE ME SEERIOUSLY
Well that should raise some eybrows in the gay community
FUCK YOU, FAGS. YOU DON'T OWN ME.
XXX

AND TIM
IF YOU'RE OUT THERE, IF YOU REALLY LOVED ME, YOU'D CALL ME BACK
I MEAN, ONE FUCKING PHONE CALL IS THAT SUCH A
OH SHIT.
SMITHS
Can you edit that out?
Maybe, if you're very, very nice to me.
TIME

SO MR. MACHINE WHY DO YOU HAVE SUCH A PERFECT ASS?
"SHIT. DOUG. YOU PROMISED"

How Do You know? Did You Talk To Tim? What else did he say about me?
I guess you don't remember our little evening together at the viper room?
DOUG TREVOR
DOUG TREVOR
SNIFF
SNIFF
The Welcome Mate Out!
FRUIT OF THE LOOM 32
Oh Right.
XXX
OKAY, UH, IT'S PERFECT BECAUSE YOUR DICK HAS NEVER BEEN ANYWHERE NEAR IT.
nice one, Trevor.
THANKS!

VINNIE
BARBARINO
Anyway, "The Dam," your song about River Phoenix looks to be an anthem for this generation. Do you want to talk about it?
ARRAH
AWCETT
AJORS
Uh...yeah, well, I relate to River, you know? He was too honest and uncompromising for this world, and so am I. And, uh... when I sing that song, I become River. He's speaking through my, uh... imagination or whatever.
RING!
Does that make sense?
RING
!
HELLO?
Oh, hi, Dad.

RIVER
RIVER
RIVER

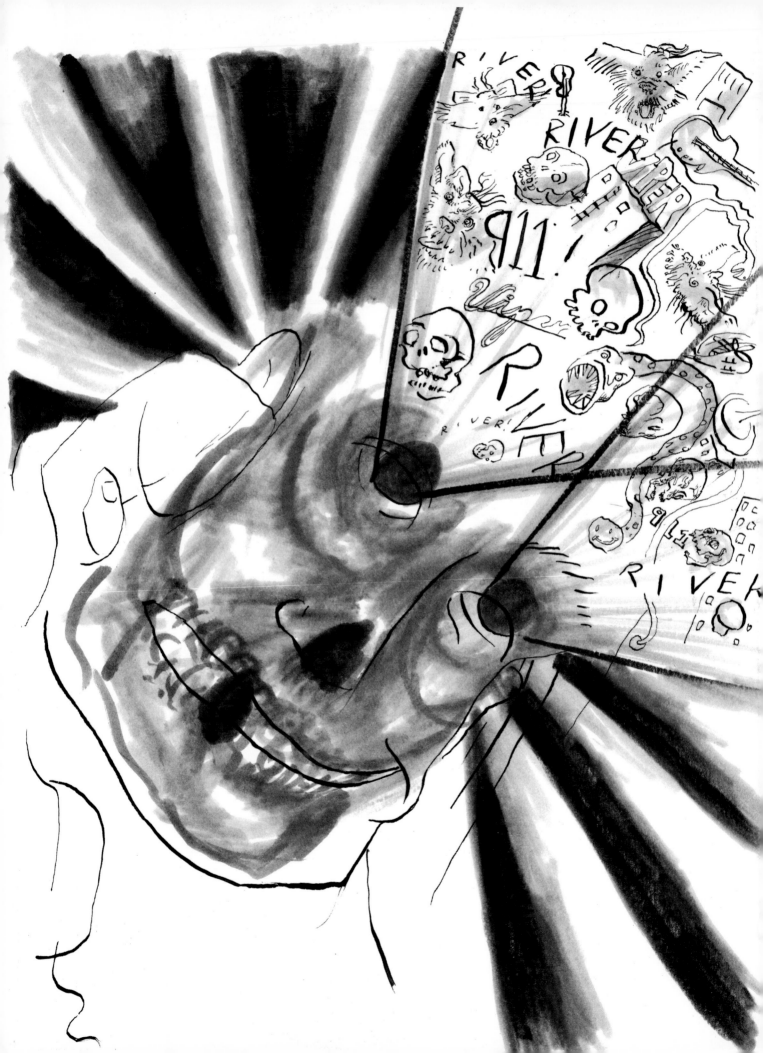

MA
I ♡ KIMBA

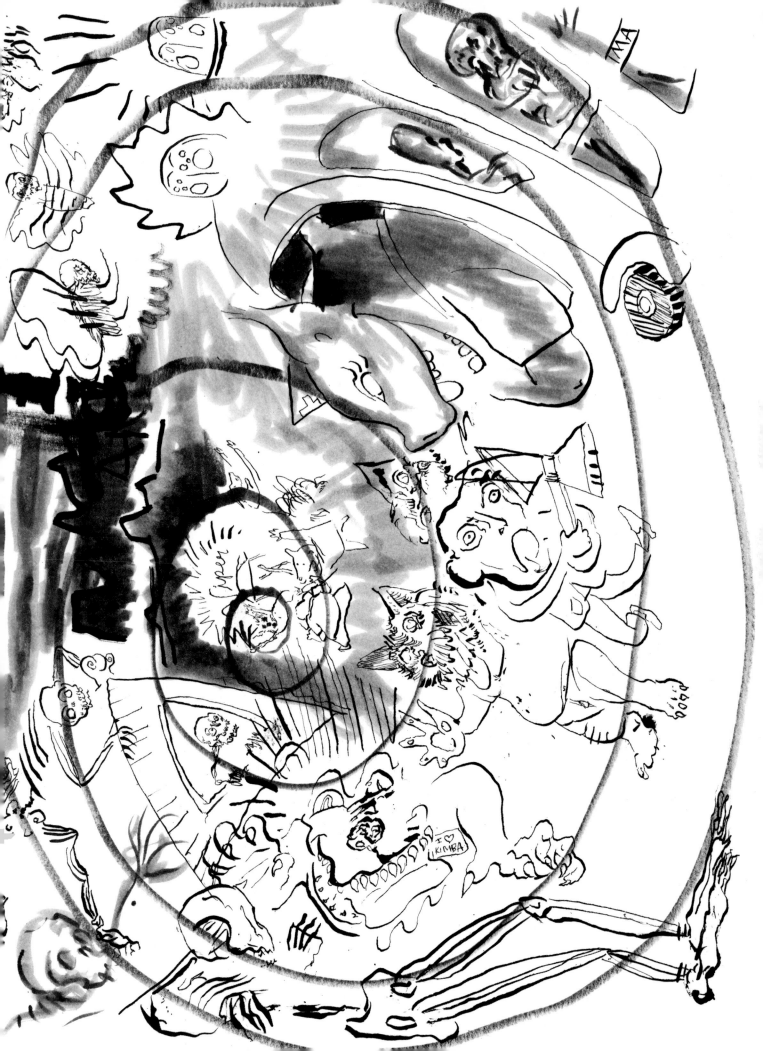

I HAVE SOMETHING TO TELL YOU...

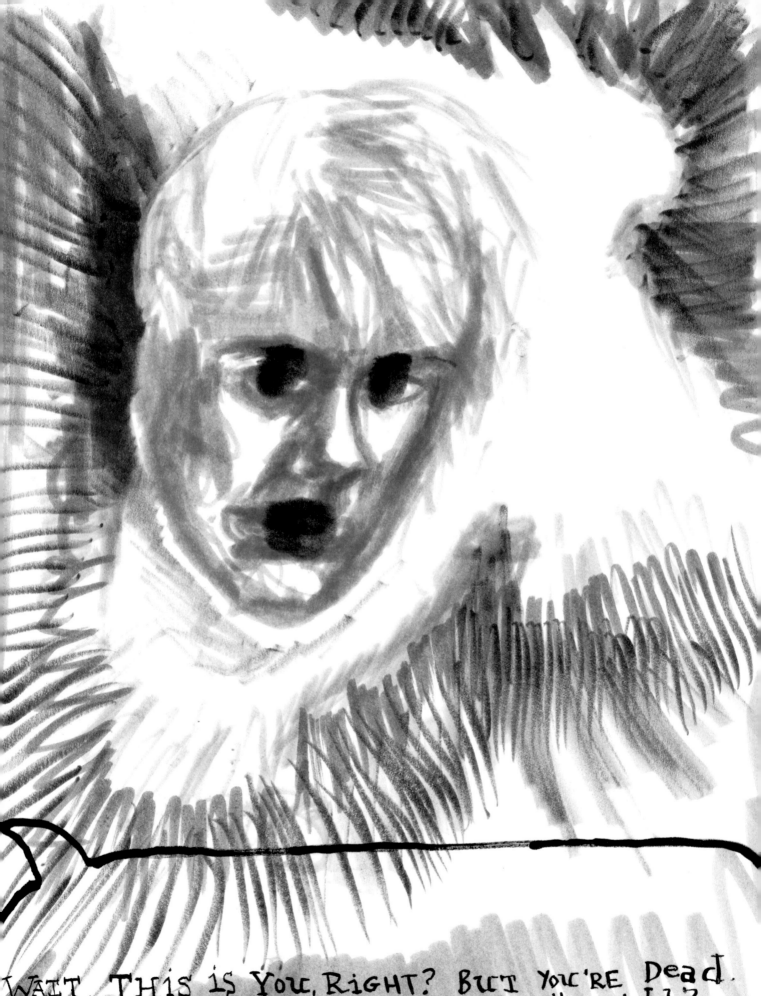

WAIT. THIS IS YOU, RIGHT? BUT YOU'RE DEAD. So~~u~~ you're a ghost, right?

IN LAYMEN'S TERMS.
LISTEN, I APPRECIATE YOUR SONG ABOUT ME.
I LIKE IT,
and I think it's sincere.

I WANT TO PAY YOU BACK BY GIVING YOU SOME INFORMATION THAT ONLY THE DEAD CAN KNOW, BUT WHICH I THINK WILL BENEFIT YOU.
COOL. WOW. THANKS.

FIRST OF ALL, DON'T RUIN YOUR
THOSE RECORD COMPANY ASSHOLES. AND TELL HIM YOU LOVE HIM.

RELATIONSHIP WITH TIM. GO OVER TO

OLOGIZE FOR SLEEPING WITH

AND DO IT PRONTO.

HIS APARTMENT AND AP

OK. GOD, THIS IS SO WEIRD.

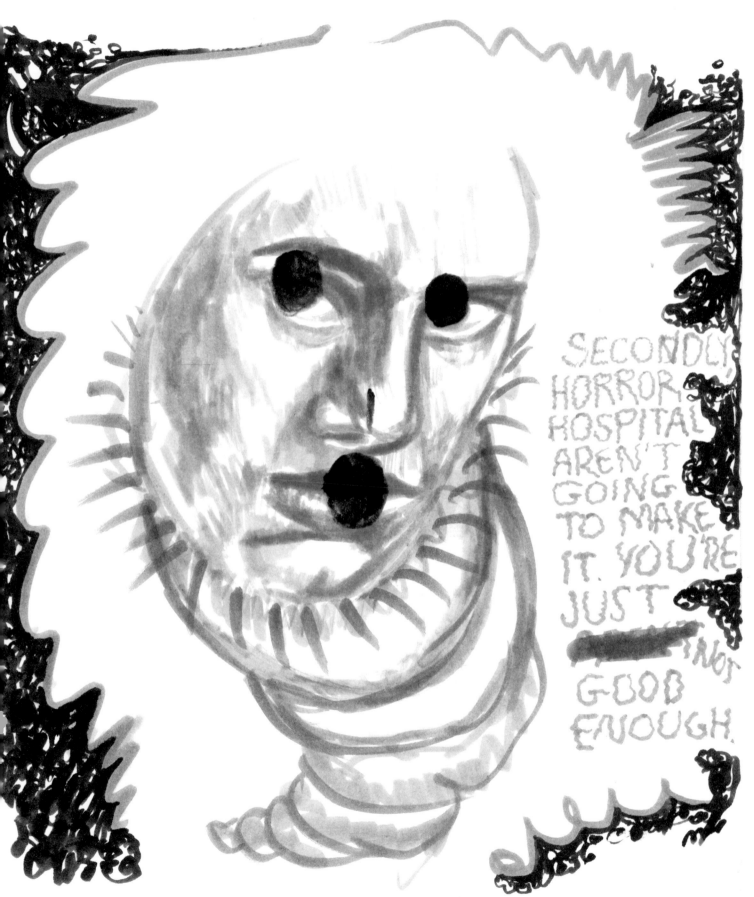

SECONDLY.
HORROR
HOSPITAL
AREN'T
GOING
TO MAKE
IT. YOU'RE
JUST
NOT
GOOD
ENOUGH.

REALLY? FUCK. OKAY, OKAY.

FINALLY. I HATE TO TELL YOU this, but in twelve days and seventeen hours from now you're going to die of an accidental drug overdose, just like I did

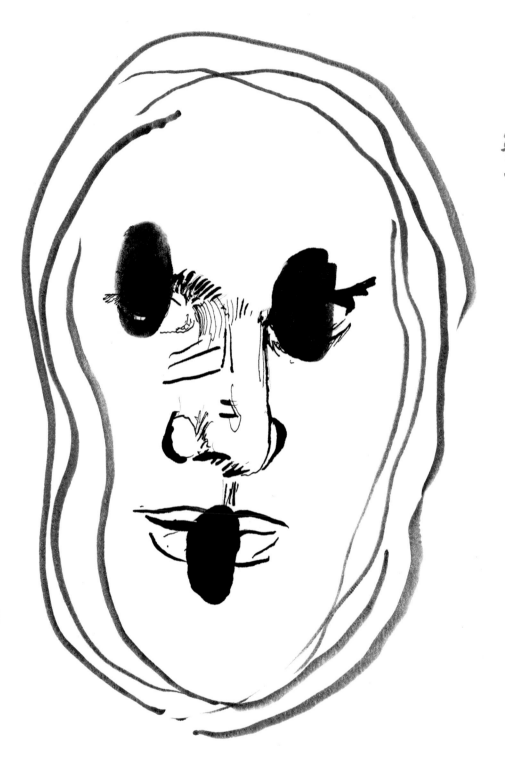

I tell you this so you won't ~~anymore~~ go do what I did and blow your last couple of weeks.

AND IF it's
any consolation,
death's not
so bad.

It's kind of laid back.

Oh,
shit.

NOW GO
TREVOR

BURN O
BRIGHTLY

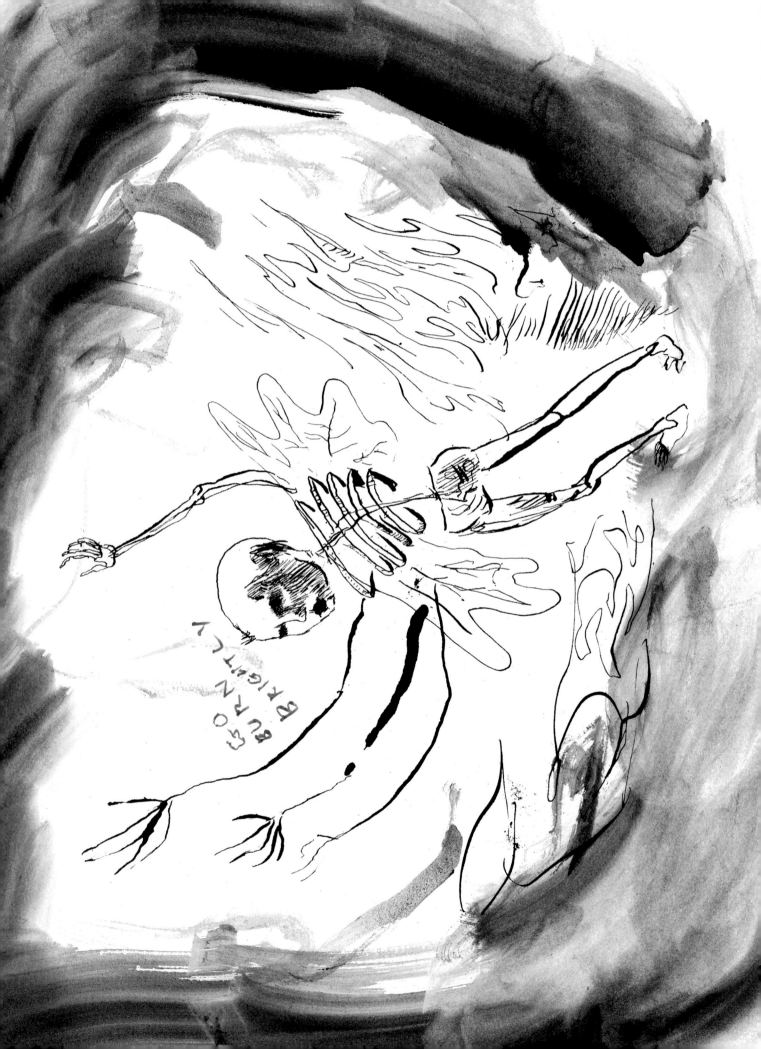

and fuck with the world
NIKE

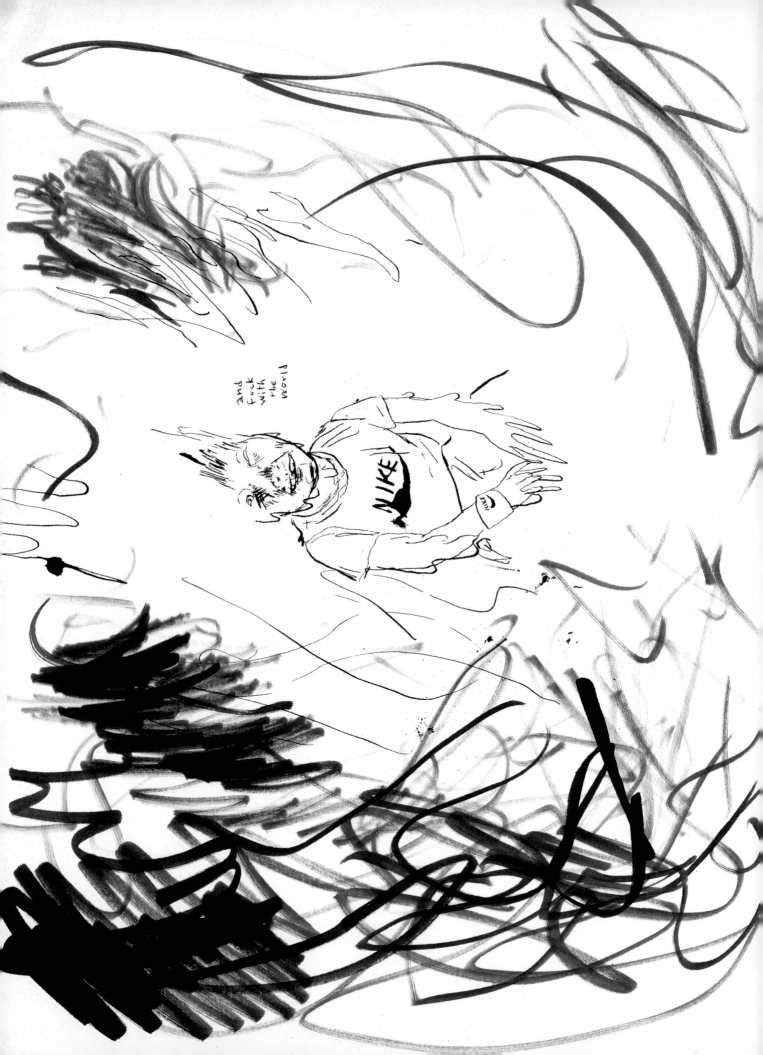

IN A BEAUTIFUL WAY.

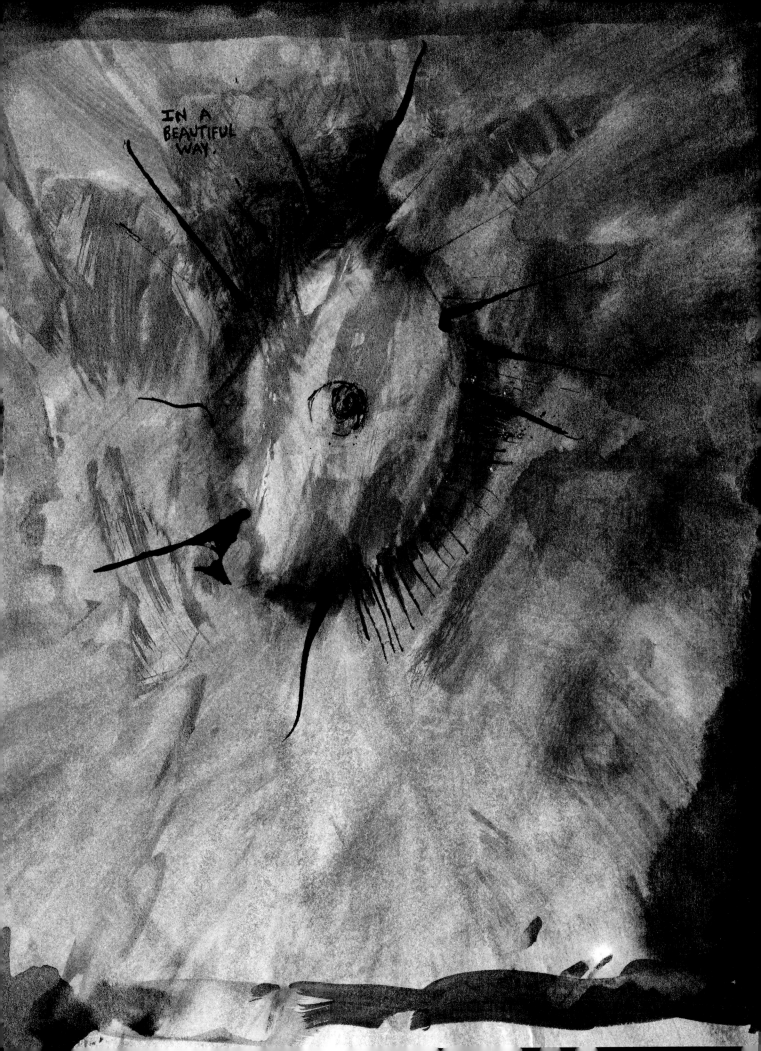

Uh, I have to go, Dad.
I think I just had an acid flashback.

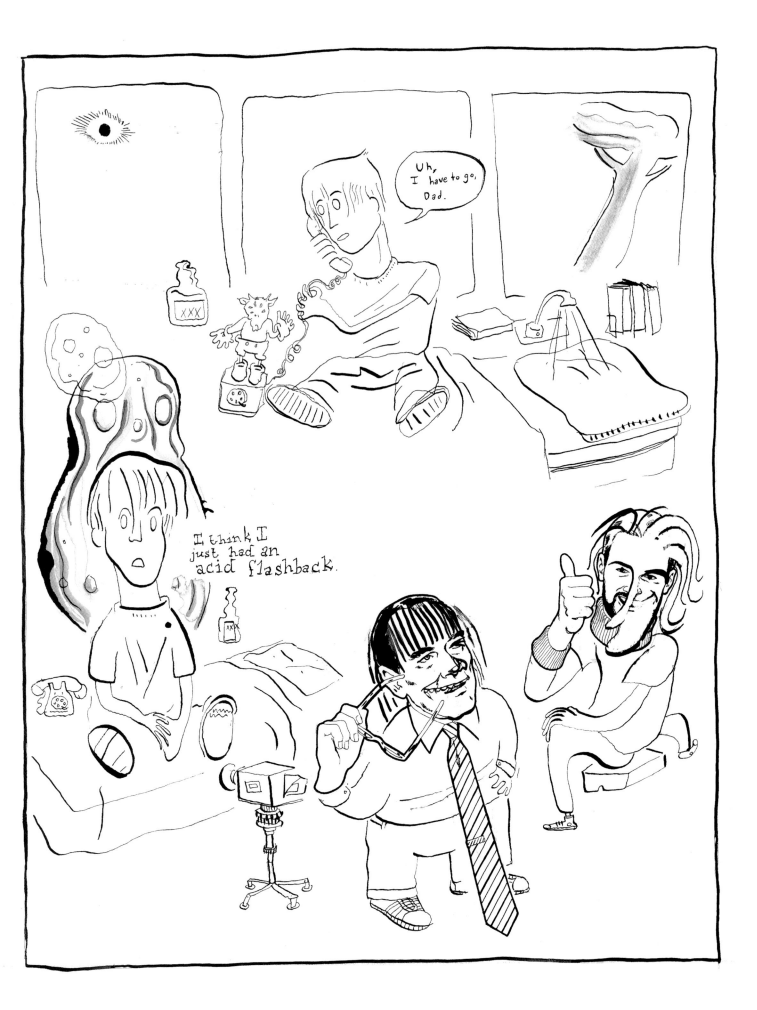

you do have a really weird look on your face
What was it like?
PAUL SMITH
PAUL SMITH
I saw River Phoenix. I talked to him. Or I mean, he talked to me.

WAS HE NAKED?
I...
don't remember.

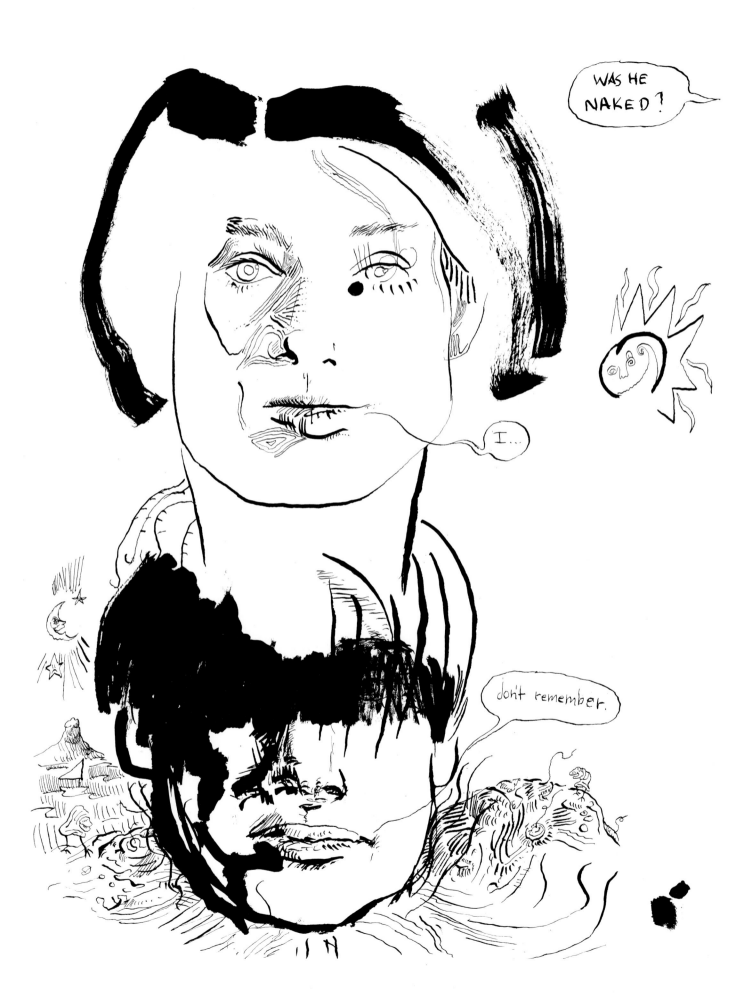

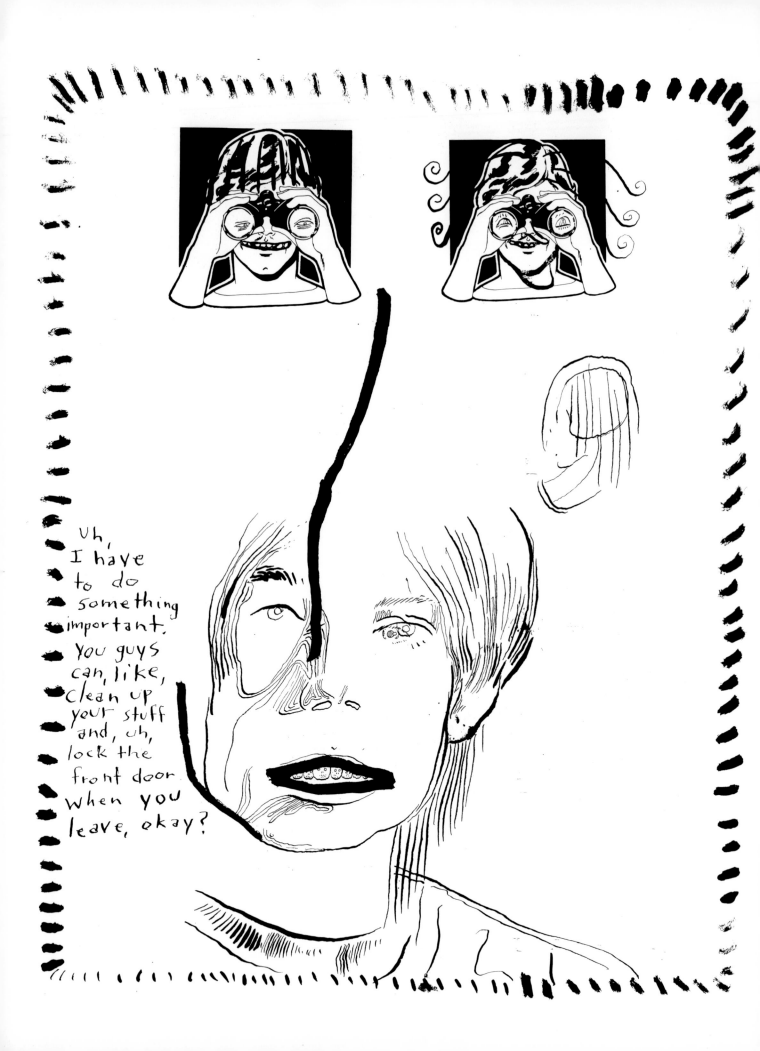

Uh,
I have
to do
something
important.
You guys
can, like,
clean up
your stuff
and, uh,
lock the
front door
when you
leave, okay?

YOU CAN INTERVIEW ME AGAIN TOMORROW OR WHATEVER YOU WANT TO OKAY?
SLAM!
Ever since Trevor got that call from David Geffen, he's been on this obnoxious star trip
The Trevor Machine Souvenier Shop is open for business.

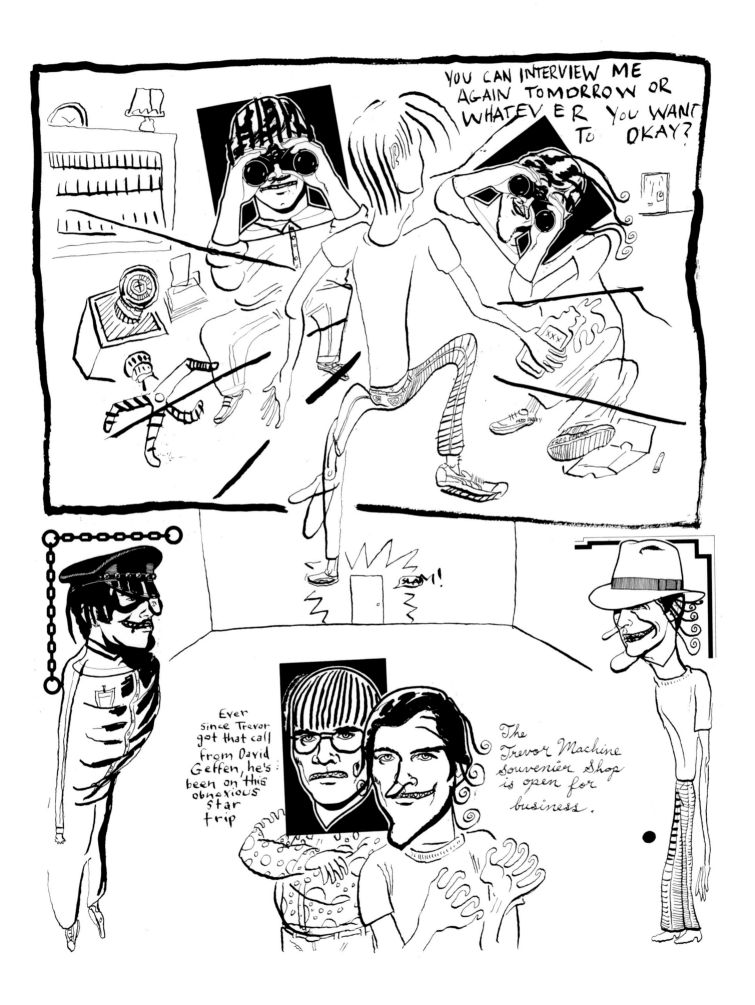

SCORPIAN WORLD
BEING & NOTHINGNESS
CUJO
IN YOUTH IS PLEASURE
the Bears and I

BOWIE
Hey, Doug, I thought you were over Trevor. Aren't you going out with Devan?
We fucked a couple of times
the "Loot"
But Devan's a little too kinky for me.
bong water
bong
If you can imagine that.
CANDY UNDERWARE
FOR MAN WHO HAS EVERYTHING
FOR BK
CHINESE HANDCUFFS
condom

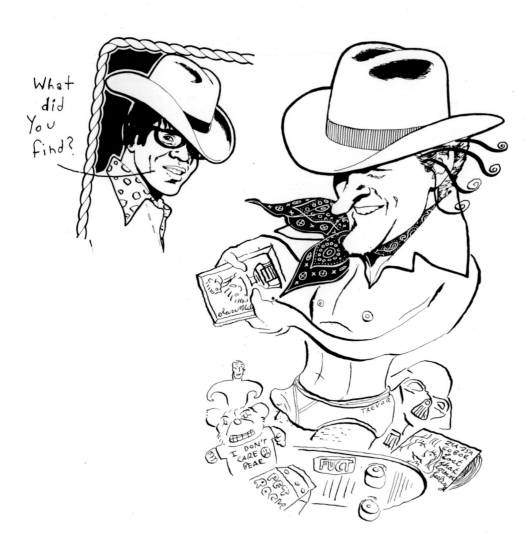

What did you find?

Trevor's six grade school portrait

Look at him.

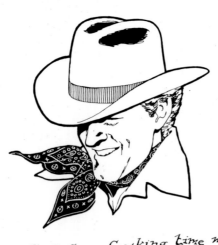

God, for, a fucking time machine.

CIGARETTE BUTT
he put his lips around this.
'Nuff said.
He must have worn this for a month.
yum.
sock
It smells absolutely nightmarish.

Handwritten lyrics.
FUCK YOU
Le piece d'resistan
HIS COME RAG.
Oh Yeah?
YOU AND
WHA
ARMY
AND MAY I SAY, IT IS CAKED.

MEAT BALLS
ROCKY MT. OYSTER
S.T.P.
FUCK DEAD
100% KOSHER

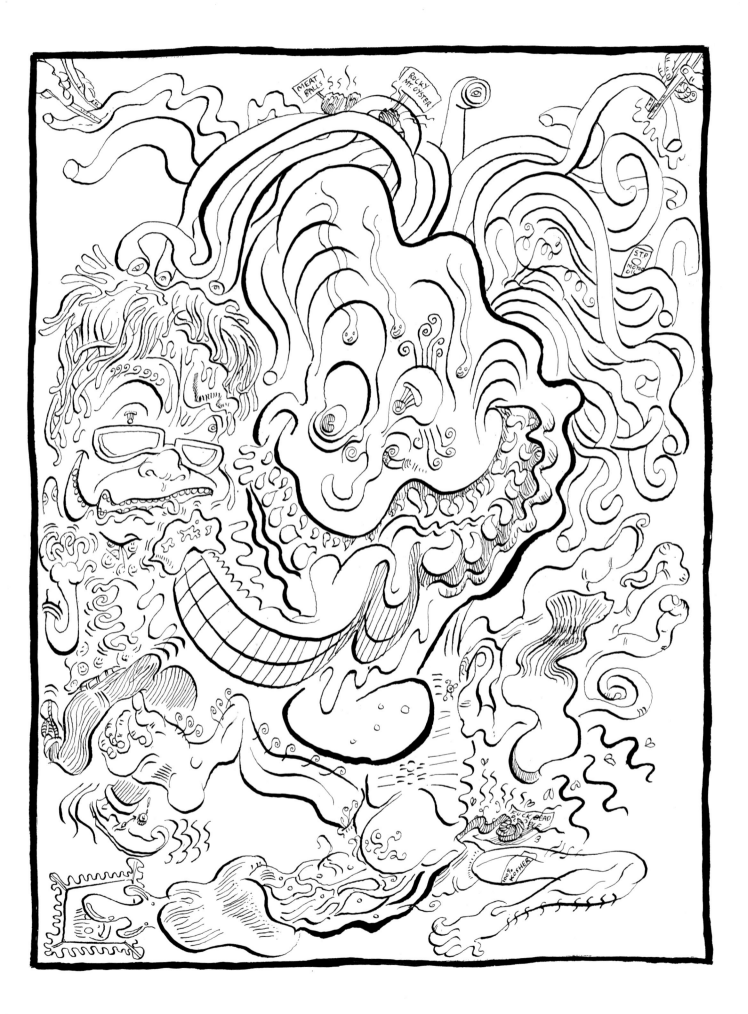

MEANWHILE, ACROSS TOWN...
IN DULL'S BEDROOM...
ANOTHER BOY WAS SLIDING UP THE HALLWAY, HE MERGED PERFECTLY WITH THE HALLWAY.
It's stupid to be in love with Trevor.
Tim... just call Trevor.
Tim...
THE BOY WAS IN THE HALLWAY DRINKING A CUP OF TEA
I'M such a pathetic fag hag.
IN KIMBERLY'S GARAGE...
BEN GAY

I know,
I know.
CRICK!
THE BOY LOOKED AT JOHNNY/ JOHNNY WANTED TO RUN/ BUT THE MOVIE KEPT MOVING/ AS HE PLANNED/ THE BOY TOOK JOHNNY/ HE PUSHED HIM AGAINST THE LOCKER/ HE DROVE IT IN/ HE DROVE IT HOME/ HE DROVE IT DEEP IN JOHNNY....
AT DEVAN'S BOYFRIEND'S BEDROOM/DUNGEON
MARIA
ALAS
DEVAN
DEVAN'S BOYFRIEND
CRISCO

WHY can't I get over this?
GOT TO LOSE CONTROL/ GOT TO LOSE CONTROL/ THEN YOU TAKE CONTROL
I have to get him off my mind somehow...
WATCH ME PULL A RABBIT OUT OF MY HAT?
AGAIN?
We're mountains.
and proud of it!
WHAT, WHAT?
I LOVE HORROR HOSPITAL
cigarette
nipple
OH hi. I mean, hello sir.
I LOVE YOGI'S YANG
I'M FISHY!
LANGER SMITH
GIVE A HOOT, DON'T SWALLOW!
he's an irresponsible, self-involved brat...
HELLO, PIECE OF SHIT,
THINK THINK
JOHNNIE'S LAYING THERE IN HIS SPERM COFFIN
HELP ME! MORRISEY! PLEASE SAVE ME! OH GOD, HELP ME MORRISEY!
MT. Rushmore
chainsaw
WHIRRRR!!
butcher
HOLLWOODLAWN
what if Drew BARRYMORE SUDDENLY WALKED INTO THE DOOR AND SAID
OKAY
DO YOU KNOW HOW TO PONY LIKE BONEY MARONEY
DO YOU KNOW HOW TO TWIST WELL IT GOES LIKE THIS
TWISTER, LIKE YOUR BABY SISTER
hey did you do...
I THINK YOU REMEMBER PERFECTLY WELL...
KIMBERLY, I THINK I'M DYKE CAN YOU HELP ME FIND OUT
TWIST THE
DO THE ALLIGATOR / AND YOU

I GUESS I DIDN'T KNOW MY OWN STRENGTH!
I'M CANADA!
NOW! HERE'S SOMETHING WE HOPE YOU'LL REALLY ENJOY!
hmm!
I'm a great lake!
a greased fist
What are we called again? Peninsulas?
I'M GOING TO RIGHT INTO HIS EYE!
NO WAIT, WAIT, SHE LOOKS TOO MUCH LIKE TREVOR. OH FUCK.
I'M A TREE!
NEW HAMPSTER
WE'RE EVIL CORPORATE GIANTS
WASH. D.C.
No - I think it's pituitary gland!
GET THE FUCK OUT OF HERE!
SWISS CHEEZE
HEY MORRISEY HEY! HELP ME OUT!
ALL RIGHT! I'M A TREE! WOOO!
So what goes on in the mid-west nowadays? I mean, I feel so disconnected here somehow.
oh yes? Well I'm a golf course.
no big deal! just some suburbs!
I know what you mean. That's why I'm moving to N.Y.
black sheep
I'M A MALL!
I'M FROM CINCINNATTIE!
I REPRESENT THE HOMLESS AND EMPORVRISHED IN WHAT WAS ONCE A GREAT COUNTRY.
GIVE ME A DOLLAR.
I LIKE IT LIKE THAT
YOU LIKE IT LIKE THAT
That would be PERFECT.
Yeah.
but he's cool, and he's flipping out and drinking and doing drugs,
THE COCKRING CAPITAL OF THE WORLD!
I know he was an asshole to you.
I'M A FARM! ACTUALLY I'M JUST A COVER UP FOR A POT PLANTATION BUT PLEASE DON'T TELL ANYBODY! SPECIALLY NOT THE F.B.I.!
we're wild flowers!
OUR NATION'S CAPITOL
I FORGET WHO I AM OR WHY I WAS IMPORTANT!
HOWDY! I'M MINNIE PEARL! I'M A LESBIAN!
Or if it was Winona Ryder.
THERE'S A LITTLE PLACE
THE PLACE IS CALLED SPACE ITS A PRETTY LITTLE PLACE
Hi Y'all! I'M DOLLY PARTON!
AND I'M SUZANNE SUMMERS!
TEXAS-SIZED DILDO
It ain't big enough.
did you read all the Marginalia cartoons? why?
GO JOHNNIE GO AND DO THE WATOOSIE!
J.F.K.'s BRAINS
yeah, that'd be...
HI. I'M HUCKLEBERRY HAMSTER
I YAM POPEYE!
BUT I AIN'T NO SWEE'PEA.
GOOCH!
I'M OLIVE OYL!
HELLO BOYS AND GIRLS WELCOME TO MY WONDERFUL
I'M ALLOTA OIL!
MICKEY FERRET
I'M WATER BUT DON'T DRINK ME I'M FULL OF SALT!
PALM TREES

NOW WHAT AM I GOING TO DO WITH YOU?
HATE
Hi! I'm a baby seal! Please don't club me!
I'm an iceburg! Can I freshen up your drink?
UP THERE THERE ARE A WALL OF POSSIBILITIES
THERE'S JUST A SEA OF POSSIBILITIES
I'M THE GREAT WALL!
MR CLEAN
HORROR HOSPITAL
I'm NELLIE!
I'M BIG BEN!
oh yeah? Well I'm the EIFFEL TOWER.
I'm backstroking across the channel!
FUCKA YOUSE GUYS! I'M A THE FUCKING LEANING TOWER OF FUCKING PISA!
I used to be the U.S.S.R. but now I don't know who I am!
I'm a body of water!
I'm HONG KONG! see ya leter!
but emotions are really hard for him, and...
WHAT'S THE POSSIBILITY OF A THREE-WAY WITH THAT KID IN THE MIDDLE?
You mean with Trevor? Well, he's been really depressed lately so maybe he'll go for it.
wow, sex with Trevor. What a weird idea.
where are my keys?
over here
Just who do you think you are?
I'm a WHALE and I'm PROUD
I'm the deserted island in all the New Yorker cartoons!
THERE IS A SEA! HE SEES THE POSSIBILITIES
THERE IS A SEA UP THERE
THERE IS A SEA UP THERE! THERE IS A SEA UP THERE
JAMBO!
BWANA!
I mean, What a weird idea, Sir.
I'm the Planet Earth!
and I'm Evil!
I'm South America!
I'm Salsy!
NOW WITH A PINE-FRESH SCENT!

I DIED ON THAT TOWER OF BABEL
sir?
I HOLD THE KEY TO THE SEA OF POSSIBILITIES
HI I'M VENUS! I'M THE PLANET OF LOVE! TEE-HEE!
Can you... uncuff me?
HI! I'M MERCURY! GOOD THING I REMEMBERED MY COPPERTONE!
HE OPENS HIS THROAT HIS VOCAL CORDS STARTED SHOOTING LIGHT
Shit!
I'm mysterious MARS.
I'M HALLEY'S COMET! ONE OF THESE DAYS I'M GONNA CRASH INTO EARTH AND KILL YOU ALL!
I'M EARTH! AND I'M STILL EVIL!
OH SHIT! What time is it? I have to be somewhere—
I'll talk to you later.
I've got to go, Tim. Call Trevor, okay?
SHIT
HEARD THAT CRY
SO HIGH-PITCHED THAT NOBODY
I'M VENUS! BOY WAS I UP LATE LAST NIGHT!
I'M JUPITER! HOWDY FOLKS!
THAT BUTTERFLY FLAPPING IN HIS THROAT
I'm going to be late!
NOBODY HEARD
MAKE IT SO.
CIGARETTE!
SSSSSS
HEY, I'M NEPTUNE!
AND I'M PLUTO! ARF!

ONE HOUR LATER

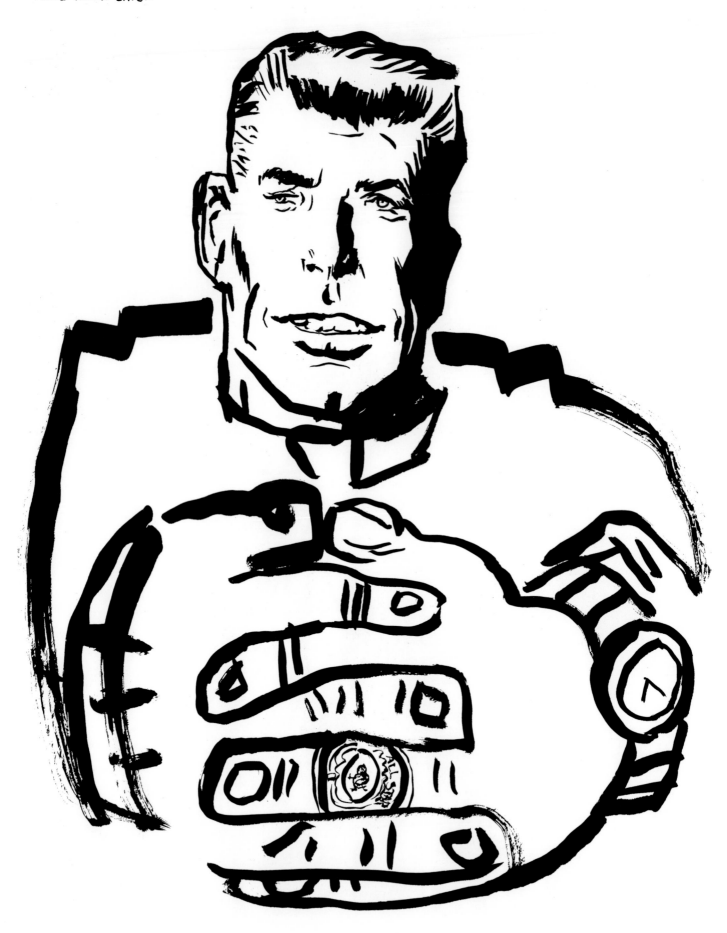

I'm sure Trevor and Devan will be here any second.

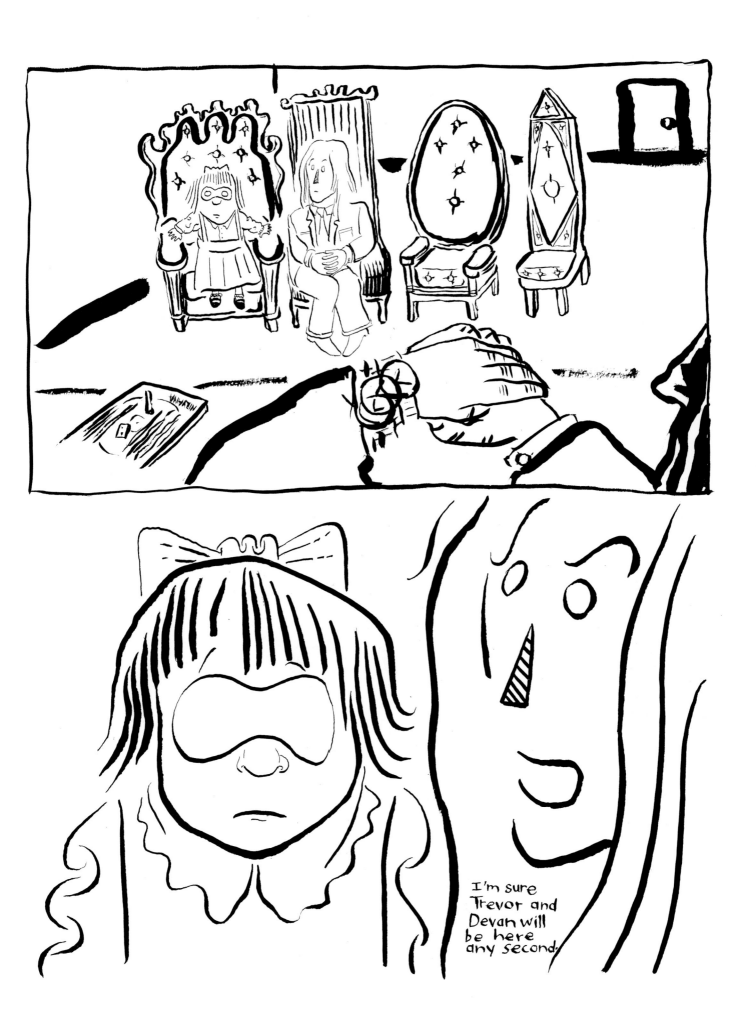

NO PROBLEM, KIDS.
THAT'S ROCK N' ROLL, RIGHT?
LISTEN, AFTER WORKING WITH GUN'S 'n' ROSES, NOTHING FAZES me.

BEEP. THURSTON MOORE ON LINE 4.
LISTEN
TALK
THANKS, BABE.
I NEED TO TAKE THIS.

HERE, HELP YOURSELF.
GOLDENSEAL ON THE LEFT, ECHINACEA ON THE RIGHT.
GO WILD.

THURS
TON.

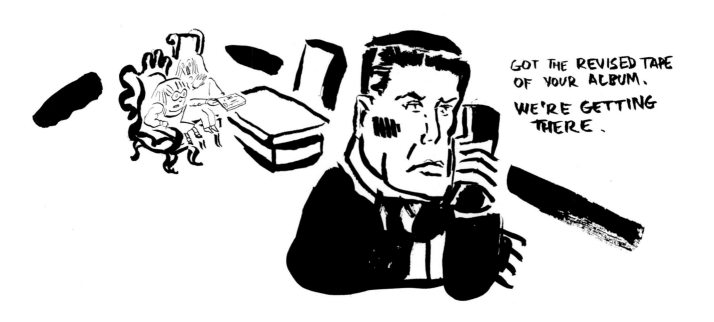

GOT THE REVISED TAPE OF YOUR ALBUM.

WE'RE GETTING THERE.

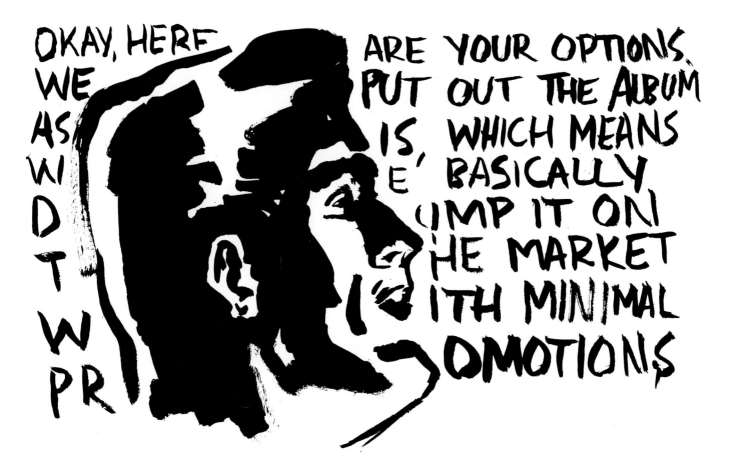

OKAY, HERE WE AS WI D T W PR

ARE YOUR OPTIONS. PUT OUT THE ALBUM IS, WHICH MEANS E' BASICALLY MP IT ON HE MARKET ITH MINIMAL OMOTIONS

OR YOU CLEAN IT UP A LITTLE, THEN WE'LL TALK ABOUT GIVING IT THE PUSH THAT ALTERNATIVE ROCK PIONEERS LIKE YOURSELVES DESERVE. THINK IT OVER AND GET BACK TO ME.

PERE UBU
UFO
UNICORN
UNION
UPP
UPSETT
QUEEZE
ULTRAVOX
UNDISPUTED TRU
NIQUE
UNIVERSE CITY
PHIL UPCHU
RIAH HEAP
U-ROY
URUBAMB
Was that Thurston Moore? I mean, the Thurston Moore?
YOU GOT IT. SO LISTEN, I UNDERSTAND YOU'RE OPENING FOR DOGSTAR AT THE ALLIGATOR LOUNGE ON THE 14th. MAKE SURE I'M ON THE GUEST LIST, PLUS ONE. I'LL CHECK OUT YOUR SET
THEN WE'LL TALK BUSINESS

COOL!

NIRVANA 'NEVERMIND'
BEEP THERE'S SOME-ONE NAMED DEVAN here to see you, but HE HAS, well... there's a---
SEND HIM IN

DEVAN'S BOYFRIEND
DEVAN
NIRVANA

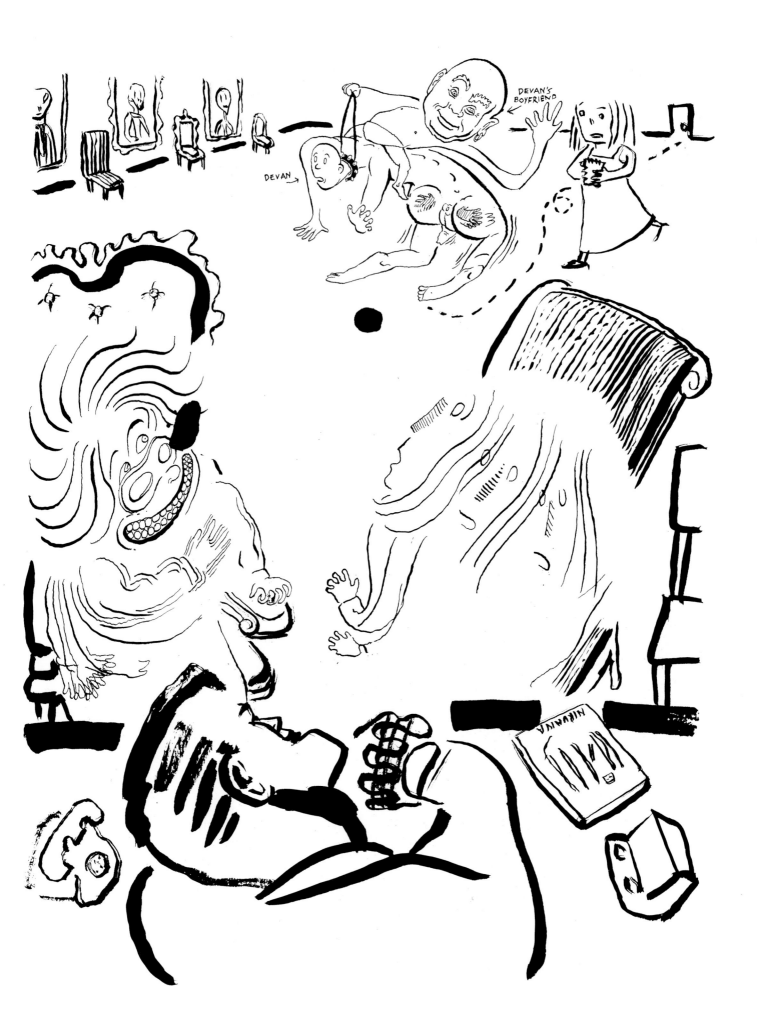

HELLO, DEVAN. QUITE AN ENTRANCE, THERE.
SIT.
GOOD BOY.
WOOF, WOOF.
NAVY
Sabu Forever
STAY.
NIRVANA

HAVE you seen Trevor?
WOOF WOOF?
Sprout forever
I GIVE GOOD (ASPARAGUS) HEAD

MEANWHILE ACROSS TOWN
Look, I'm sorry.
I FORGET THE THRILL OF IT ALL

It was just... kind of a shock.
Think how I felt?

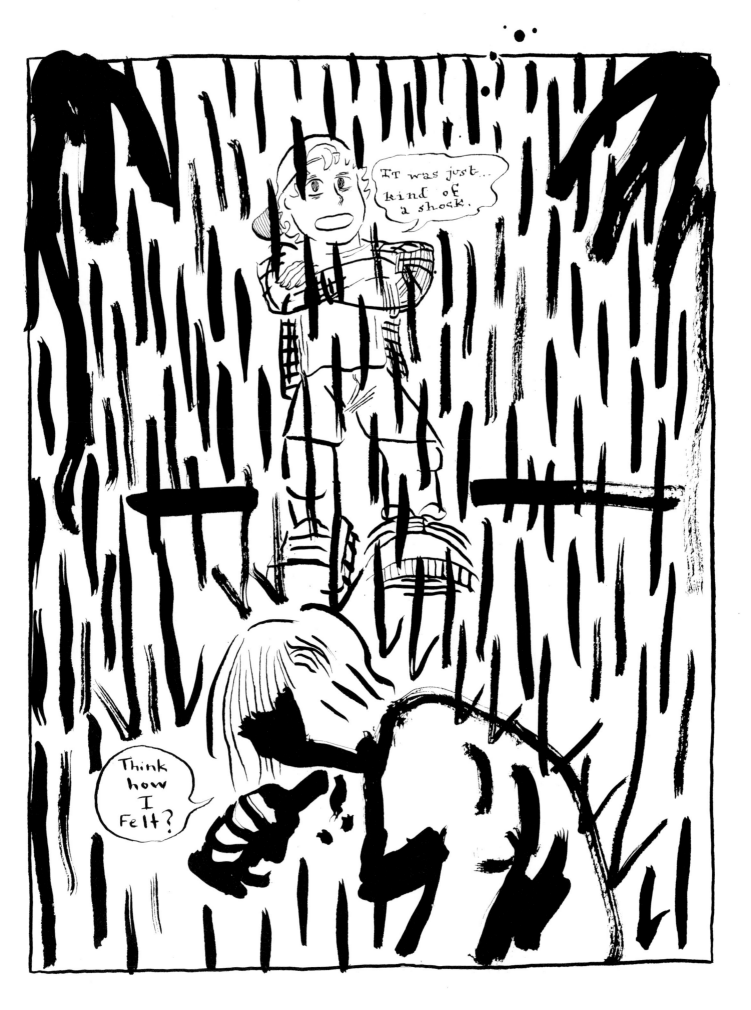

I mean about that thing at the party.
Being gay is sort of new to me.
I didn't know that there were rules and everything.
HI MY NAME IS SASQUACH

I mean, SEEING YOU STANDING THERE.

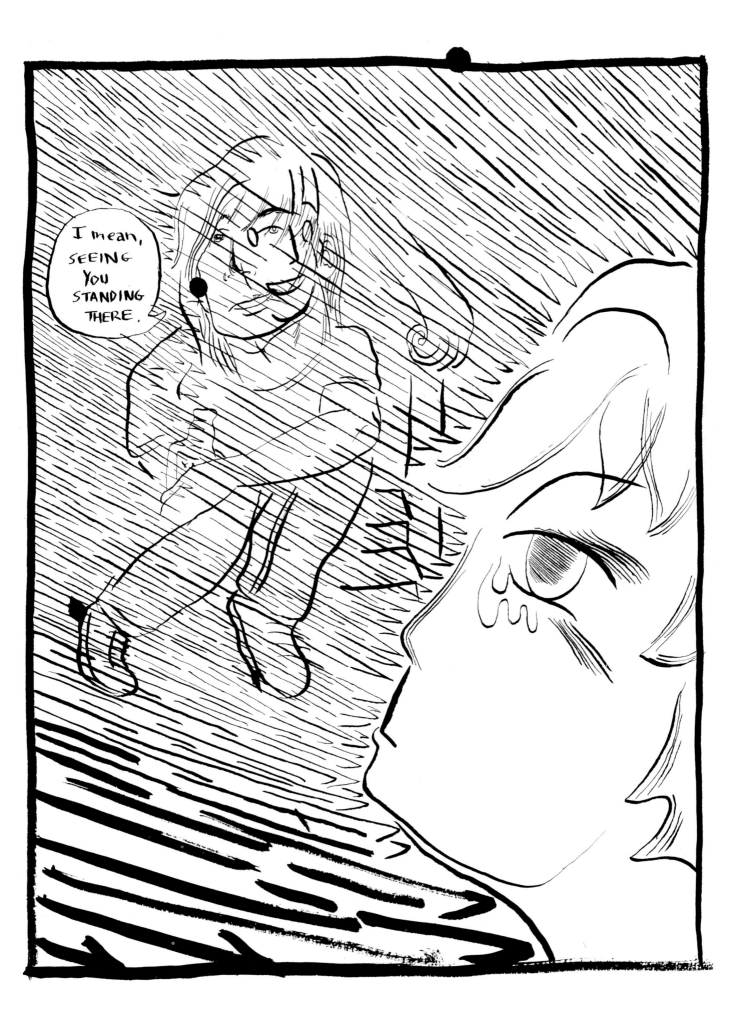

so... is stuff cool between us again?
I've been talking to my therapist about this. And she says I have [redacted] ~~be more~~ trust issues, because my parents weren't very emotionally giving. So I tend to get into this caretaker thing with my lovers, you know?

Uh... I've heard those words, like, on The Bob Newhart show and shit, but, uh, I'm not totally sure what they mean.
I need you to tell me you love me. You've never said it. I know it's hard for you, but I'm asking you to say it, as a favor to me.

uh...
I... can't
say it...

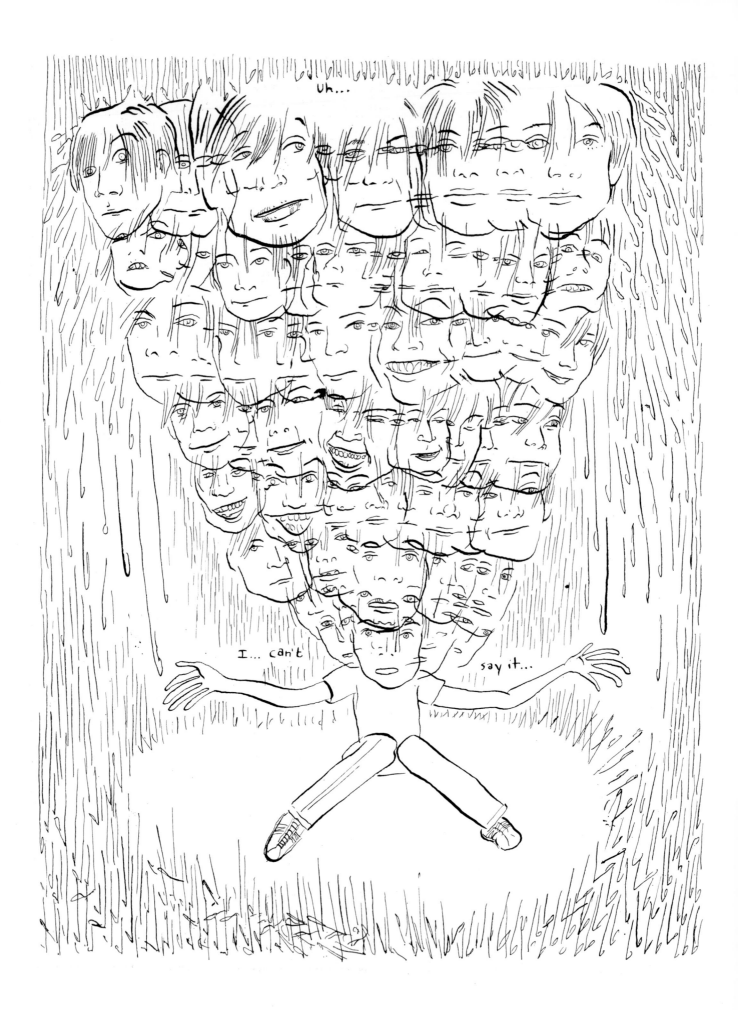

...'cos it's a, uh... I mean... Okay, look. I just read this interview with Lou Barlow in, like, I don't know, Spin, and he said, uh, something like, 'Love's not a word, it's a prison made out of language.' And I agree, you know? I just think, uh, people should do what they do, and other people should either be their boyfreind or not.
You wont say it, not even as a favor to me.
but it's a huge favor,

THEN FORGET IT!
What? Uh... I mean...
OKAY FUCK OFF

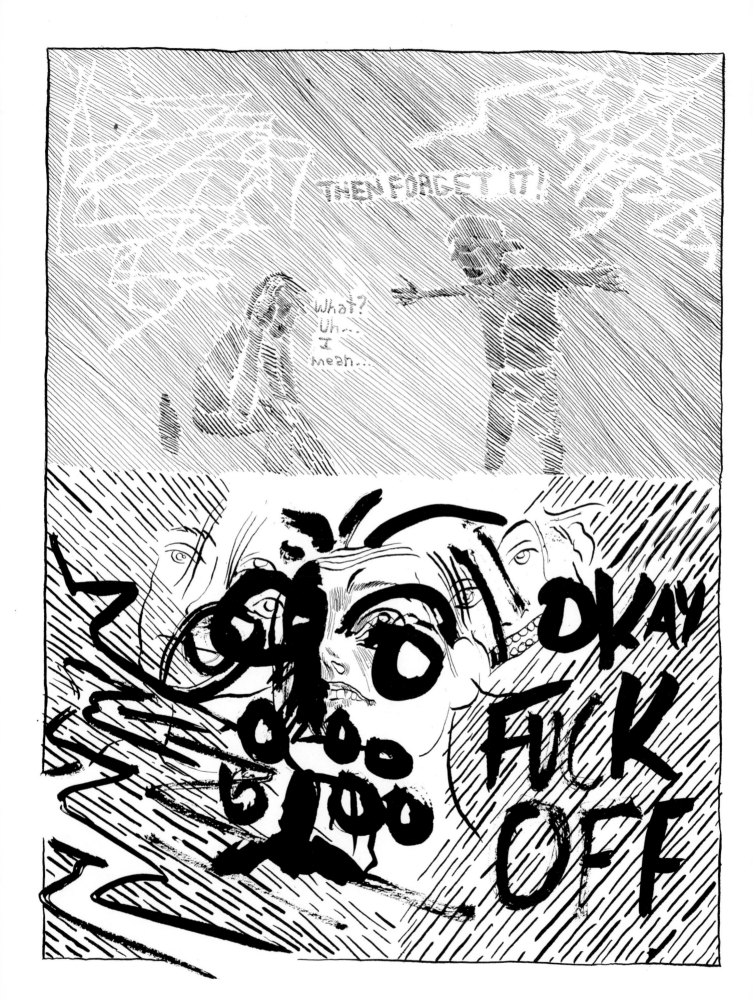

I hear you.

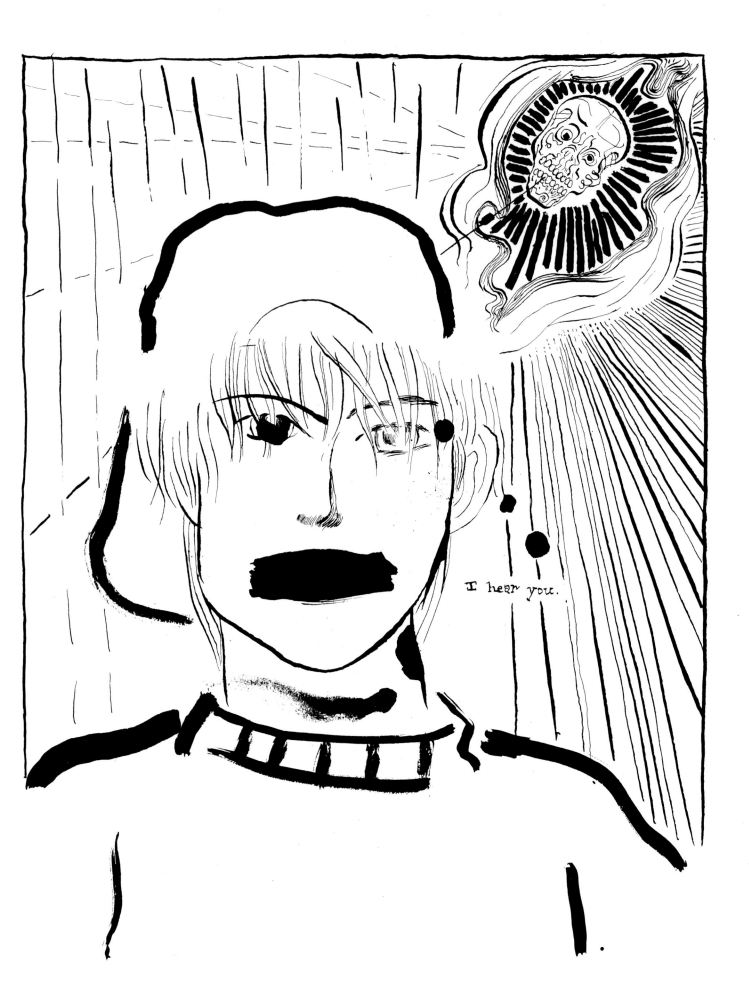

DEATH

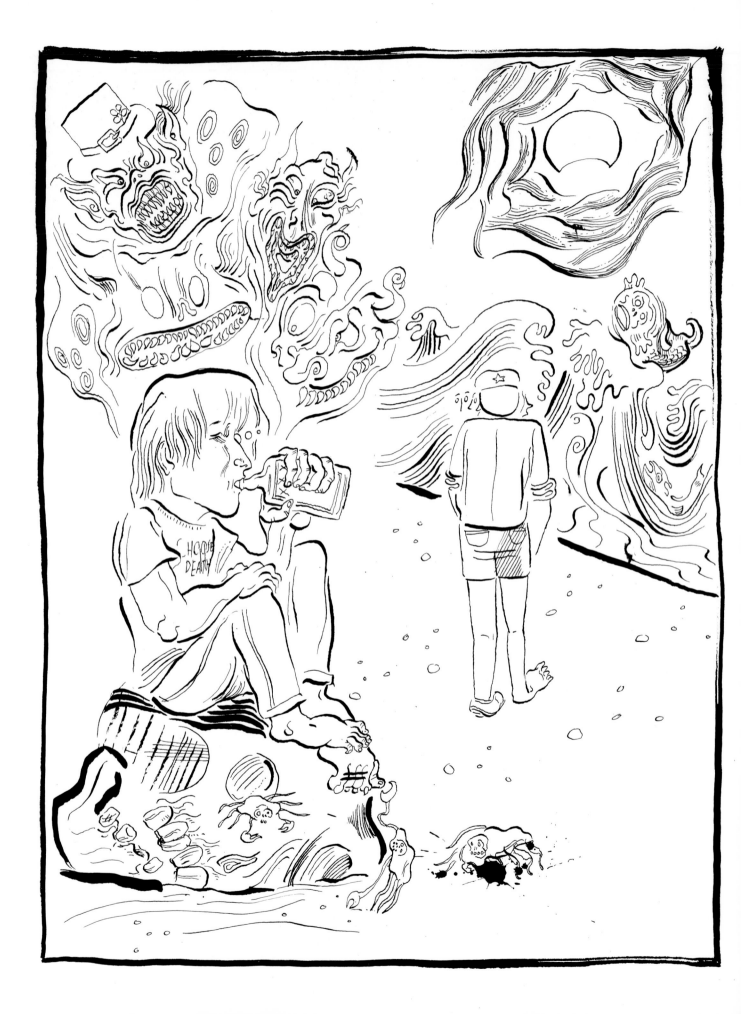

I love you, Trevor. I always will. But if you can't...

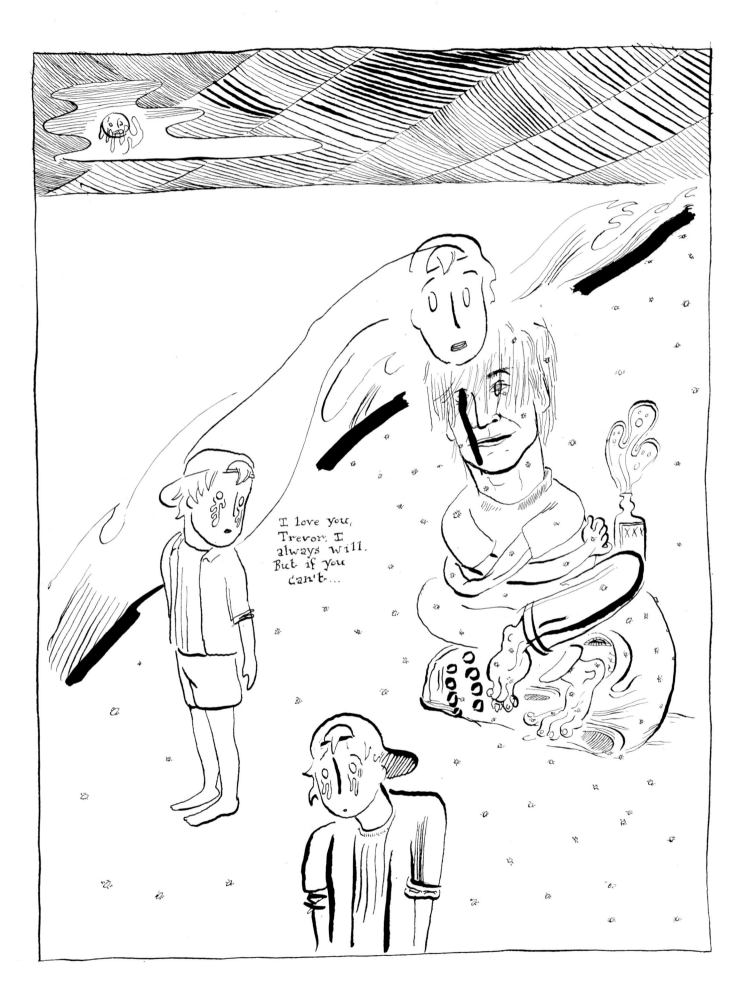

THIS
Space
for Rent

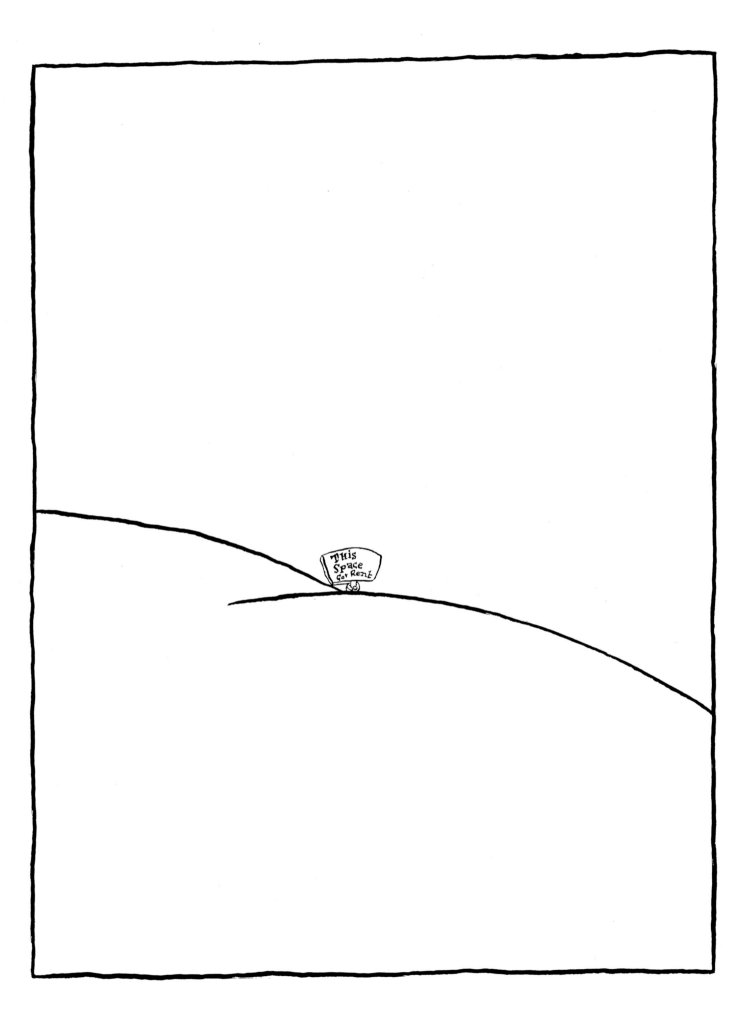

RIVER I DID WHAT YOU TOLD ME YOU FUCKING LIED TO ME!
no, I didn't

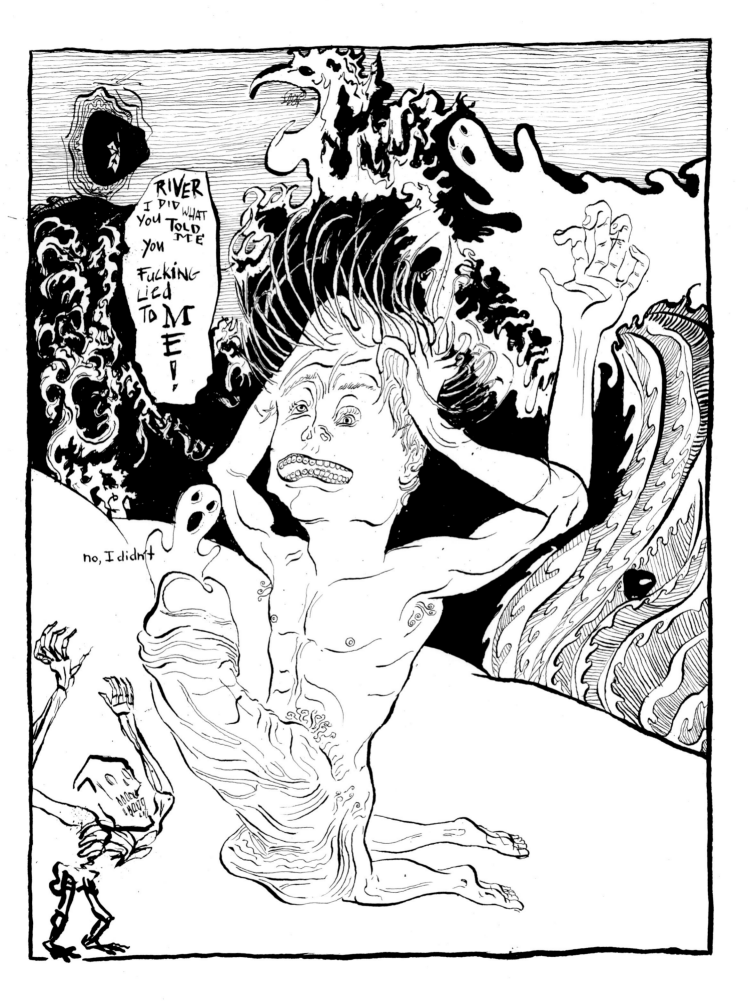

ONE WEEK LATER...

Home Sweet Home
Fuck Dead people/
Uh... I don't care/
Blah, blah, blah/
This song sucks/
This band sucks/
Who gives a shit.../
THE BIBLE, PART II

BRAVO!
BRAVO!
WHAT'S UP WITH YOU, TREVOR?
WHO CARES? WE'RE SHIT. IT'S POINTLESS!
You ruined the shot, you dork!
YEAH? WELL, YOU'RE A PENCIL-NECKED GEEKY FUCKING QUEEN!
DEVAN'S BOYFRIEND

OH, GREAT.
YES, SIR.
YOU. HERE. NOW.
XXX
JELLY
CAT SUP

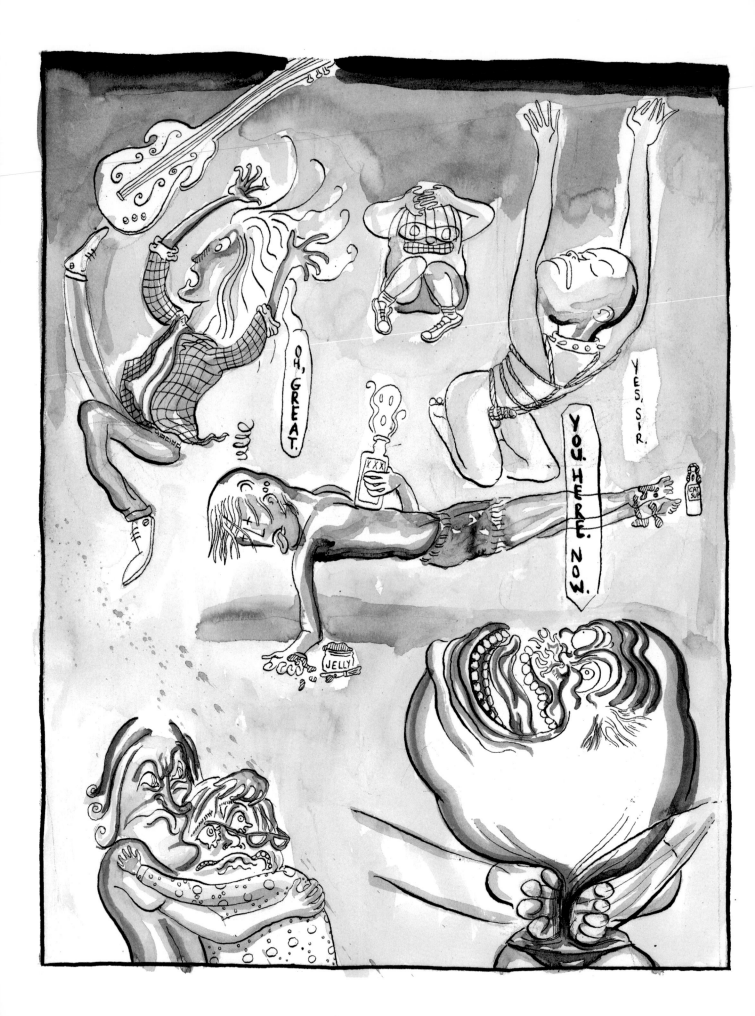

what exactly do you see in that guy?
Look... I KNOW HE'S OBNOXIOUS AND AN IDIOT,
BUT THE SEX...
PHEW.
IS THERE ANY POINT IN CONTINUING THIS?
IF THAT TREVOR KID ISN'T NAKED IN A SLING IN FIVE MINUTES...
STRANDED
PEOPLE ARE GOING TO DIE.
DON'T WORRY, SIR. TREVOR'S SO FUCKED UP HE WON'T NOTICE IF WE GO TO YOUR PLACE INSTEAD OF TAKING HIM HOME...
J. GEILS BAND
We're in good shape, Dull. Trevor just needs to sober up a little.
XXX

IF YOU FUCK THIS UP TONIGHT I'LL KILL YOU!
BORN WILD
JERRY LIMES
You can't kill me, I'm already dead.
OH MY GOD! OH MY GOD!
Hey-maybe Trevor will O.D. tonight onstage. Think about it, Frank, we'll have it all on film. THIS COULD BE A MAJOR DOCUMENTARY FILM OF OUR TIME.

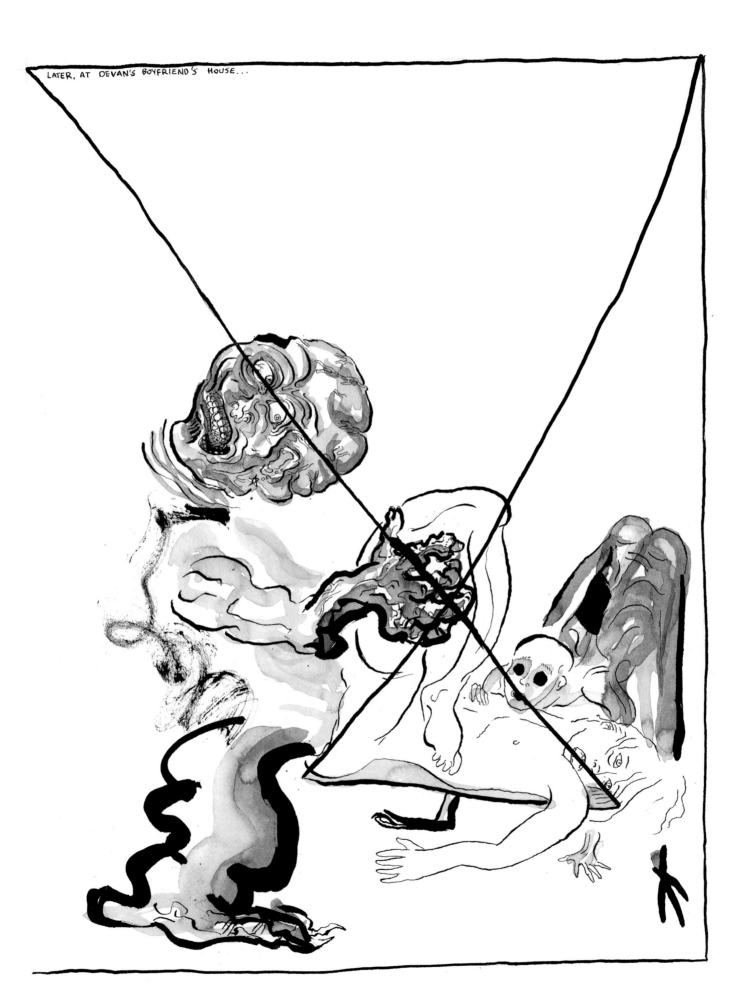

LATER, AT DEVAN'S BOYFRIEND'S HOUSE...

PASOLINI'S
DARK MASTERPIECE
NOW IN AMAZING
3D
SALO 3D
YOU'LL NEVER EAT CHOCOLATE AGAIN!
SHIT
THIS TREVOR
KIDIS A REAL
PIECE
OF WORK!
DAHMER
IN HIS FIRST ACTION-PACKED THRILLER!
"I EAT GUYS LIKE YOU FOR BREAKFAST"
TOM CRUISE · SABU
IN A MARTN SCORSESE FILM
PG-13
G.G ALLEN
"YOU WANNA TAKE IT OUTSIDE BUDDIEY?"

FELCHING · BARBARA · GYM · SALADS · CADINOX · LAGUNA BEACH ·
CHARLES NELSON RIELLY
CAN GUYS GET HARD ONS WHEN THEY'RE UNCON-SCIOUS?
KATHIE LEE'S
HARPERS
LAWN TENNIS IN THE
THIS IS CREEPING ME OUT.

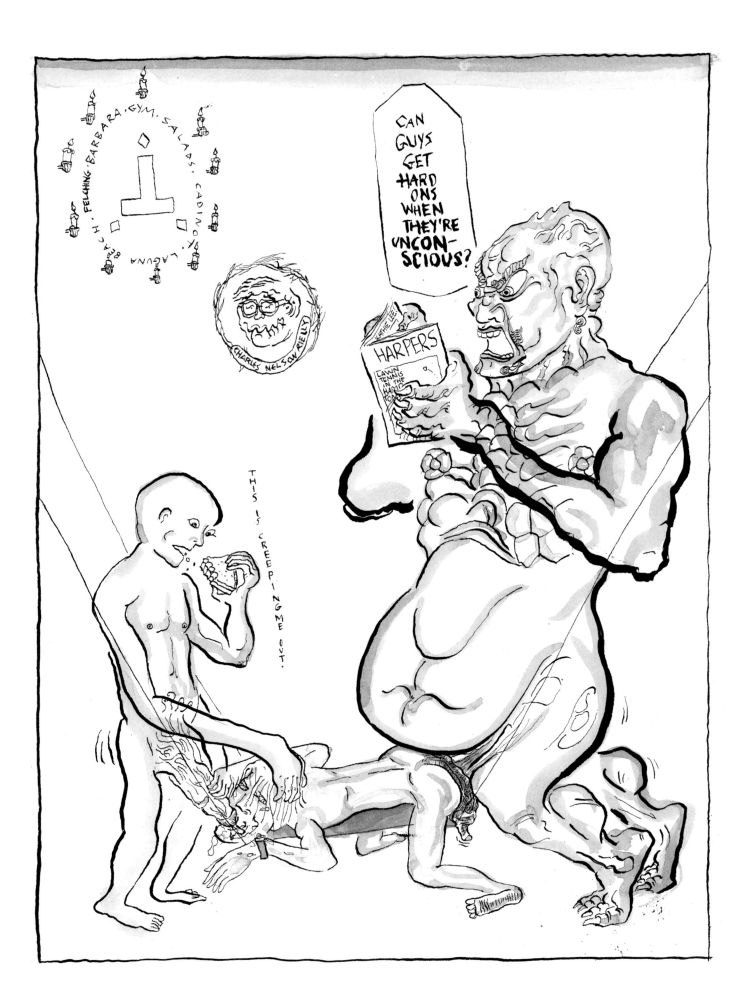

MAYBE IF I STRANGLE HIM A LITTLE.
POW! RIGHT IN THE KISSER!
STELL
THE EARTH MOVED AT FIRE ISLAND
WHAT ARE YOU TALKING ABOUT!!
LADY BIC

I'M NOT GOING TO KILL HIM, FUCKHEAD, JUST STRANGLE HIM A LITTLE.
THIS IS
TOTALLY
UNCOOL!

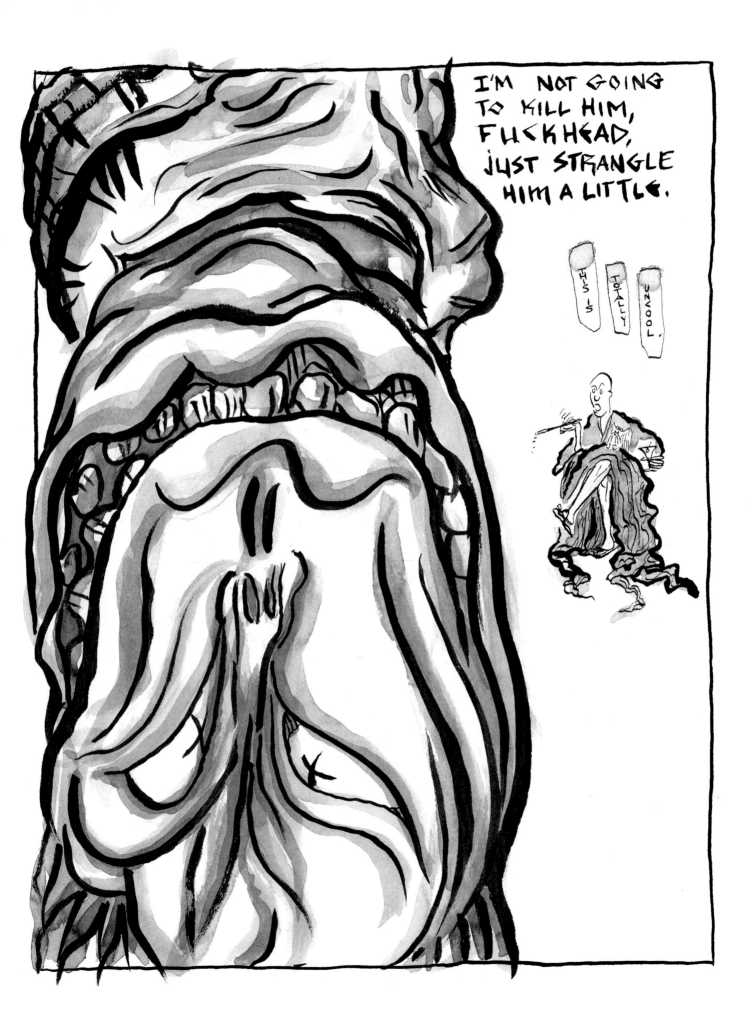

YOU'RE SUCH A FUCKING WUSS. ALLRIGHT, BOTH OF YOU GET THE HELL OUT OF HERE.
NOW.
(HIS HANDS LEAVE TREVOR'S NECK.)

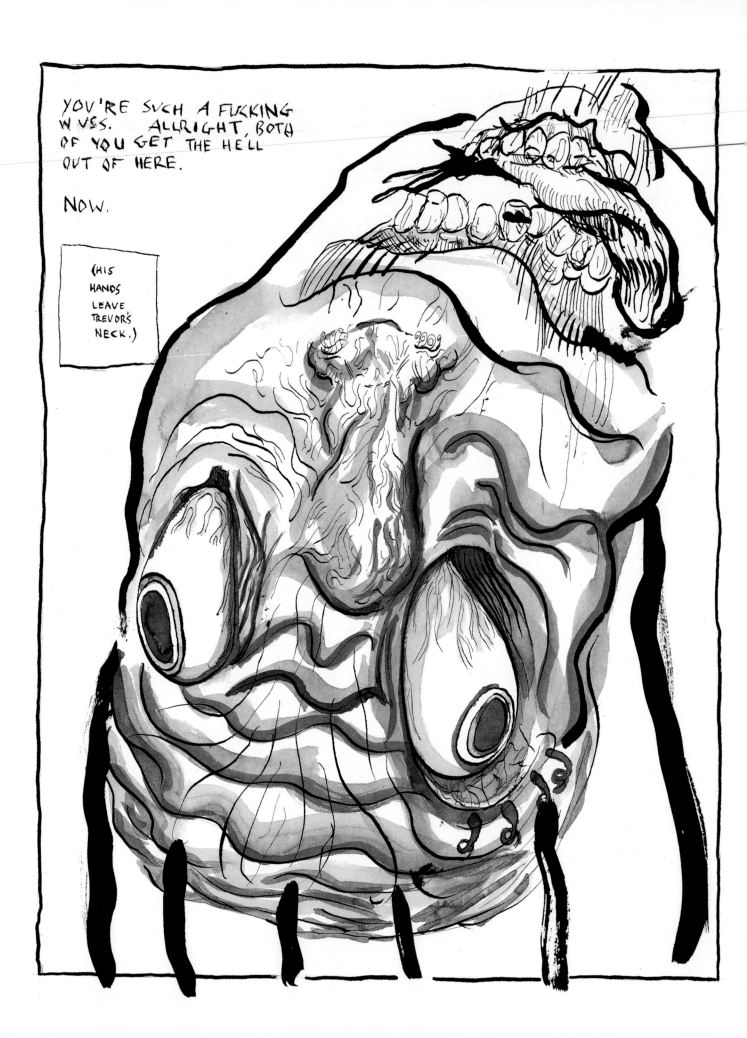

TREVOR!
WAKE UP!
WE'RE LEAVING
MM?

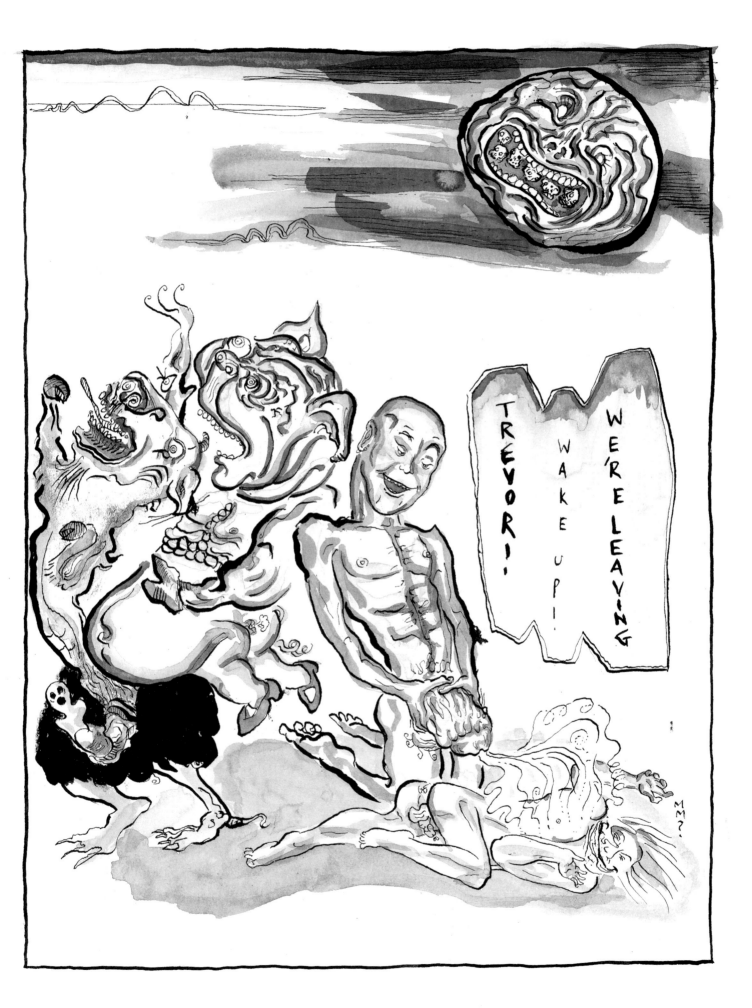

STILL LATER, AT KIMBERLY'S PLACE
26041-2
KIMBERLY'S NEW GIRLFRIEND
KIMBERLY
I'm sorry.
HI, I'M DEVAN
...and then River Phoenix just sort of, uh, disappeared, and I was back in my bedroom.
RAWHIDE
THE WAVES

So, uh, do you believe me?
Yeah, I guess so. But I don't know about that stuff about you dying in twelve days- That's... I don't want to think about that.
I'M SORRY, I'M SORRY, I'M SORRY
TREVOR, NO ONE KNOWS IF THINGS LIKE THAT ARE REAL.
IT COULD HAVE BEEN RIVER PHOENIX'S GHOST, OR IT COULD HAVE BEEN A MANIFESTATION OF YOUR SUBCONSCIOUS DESIRES.
IF YOU WANT MY ADVICE, TAKE IT AS A SIGN THAT YOU SHOULD CALL YOUR BOYFRIEND AND TELL HIM YOU LOVE HIM.
DO YOU LOVE HIM?
Yeah, I do. It's WEIRD.
I'M SORRY I'M SORRY I'M SORRY I'M SORRY I'M SORRY I'M SORRY

CALL HIM RIGHT NOW.
Shit. Uh... okay.
I'M SORRY I'M SORRY I'M SORRY
It's cool, Devan.
BEEP BEEP BEEP
It'll, uh, make a really good song.
BEEP
How about this? S&M's bullshit/ It's... uh, a fascist, uh...
Oh shit. Tim's phone machine picked up.
BE BRAVE, LITTLE PUNK.
GET TREVOR SOME MORE COFFEE, ASSHOLE.
wish

MEANWHILE, ACROSS TOWN...

WHY DON'T YOU PICK UP?
Tim, are you there? It's me. Uh.... okay Look, uh, I, uh...
My Therapist told me I should move on.
ELTON JOHN
PROUD
OUT

THEN CAN I DATE HIM?
Don't even think about it!
UH...
QUEER
I'M NOT QUEER BUT MY BOYFRIEND IS
ISN'T THAT QUEER
GRAPPLIN' WITH THE GUYS
Shit, I love you, okay? I do, I do, I do. So...
Call me back, or, uh, come to the show tonight, okay?
So...
I guess that's it.
Bye.
JUST PICK UP THE FUCKING PHONE, TIM.
OKAY...
DYING? GIVE US A TRY!
BZZZZZ
Shit. Allright, I'll call him back.
QUEER ACTING QUEER APPEARING
GENERATION QUEER
I GUESS WE SHOULD TAKE TWO CARS TONIGHT. CAN I FOLLOW YOU? 'CAUSE I DON'T KNOW WHERE THE CLUB IS.
Sure. Let's caravan
BEEP BEEP BEEPBEEP
I'M WITH QUEER
CALL NOW! GERBILS ARE WAITING! 1-800 GERE

MEANWHILE, IN TREVOR'S BEDROOM...
Trevor, it's me. I know you're there because you just called.
Okay, maybe not.
Well, thanks for the call.
I love you too.
I'll see you tonight at the show, and we can talk then.
I've missed you.
Bye.

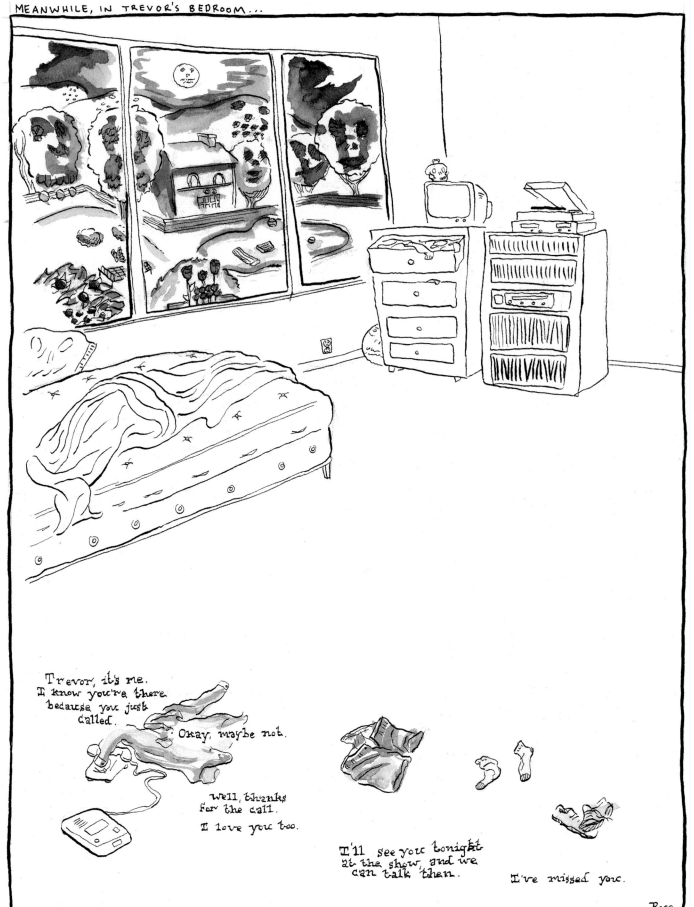

THAT NIGHT, ON THE WAY TO THE HORROR HOSPITAL GIG...
'CAUSE YOU'RE THE **DANCING QUEEN!...**
(SUNG TO THE TUNE OF DANCING QUEEN)
HORROR HOSPITAL
POW
THE HORROR HOSPITAL GIG
37 MILES THATTAWAY
Chitty Chitty bang-bang

I WAS JUST THINKING... WHAT IF HORROR HOSPITAL DON'T GET SIGNED? OUR FILM WON'T BE WORTH SHIT.
THEN WE'LL CALL IT PORTRAIT OF A BEAUTIFUL PUNK BOY AND MARKET IT AS A QUEER FILM.
YEAH, I GUESS SO.
"If a ten ton truck"*
If a ten-ton truck
* SUNG TO THE TUNE OF THE SMITHS SONG "THERE IS A LIGHT THAT NEVER GOES OUT"
mmm... Saddy!
ROCK ON!
HOLY COW
LET'S STREAK!
EVEREADY
VHS
FUCK YOU
CLINTON GORE
FCK-U AMERICA

DANCING QUEEN, FEEL THE BEAT...
FROM THE **TAMBOURINE**, OH **YEAH**!
HORROR HOSPITAL
HORROR HOSPITAL GIG THATTA-WAY
TRUCK
CALIFORNIA UPYRS LOS ANGELES
ROCK
INDIE

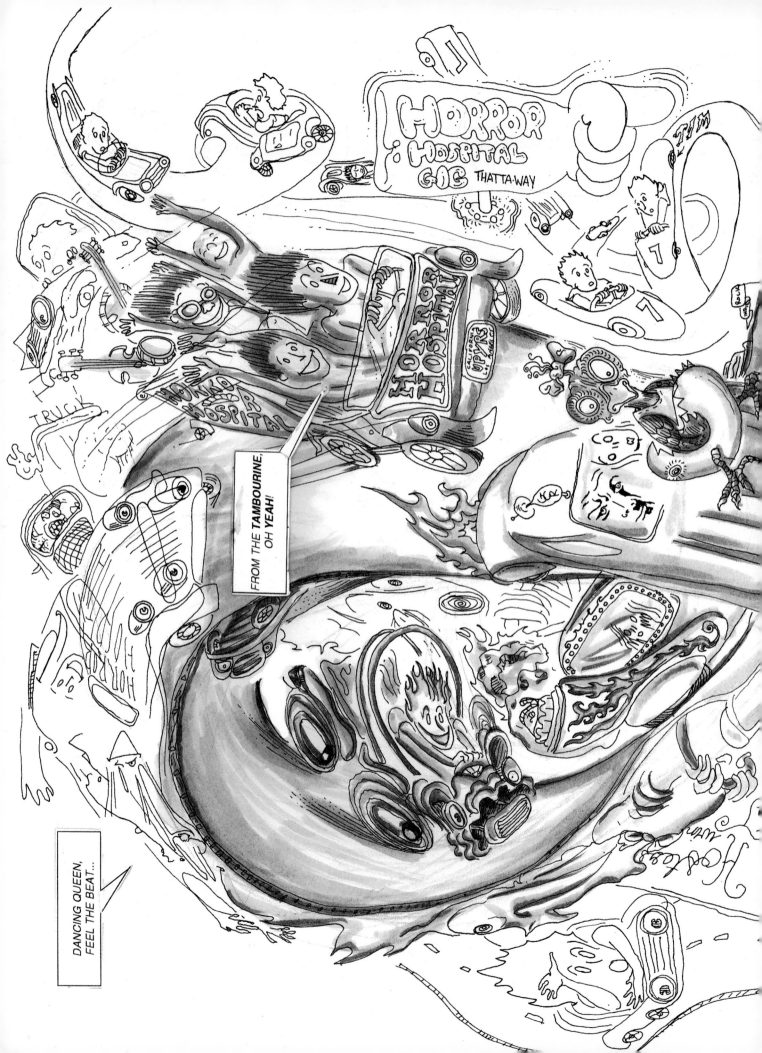

ALL I KNOW IS THAT TREVOR'S GOING TO **SIT** ON MY **FACE** TONIGHT, IF IT'S THE **LAST** THING HE **EVER** DOES.
IF HE DOESN'T **O.D.** ON STAGE FIRST!
OH, RIGHT.
NECROPHILIA. YUM.
YOU'RE SUCH A SLEAZE, DOUG.
HOT WHEELS
HONK! IF YOU LOVE PUDDIN'
MACK TRUCK
TRUCK
Truck

MEANWHILE, IN TIM'S CAR

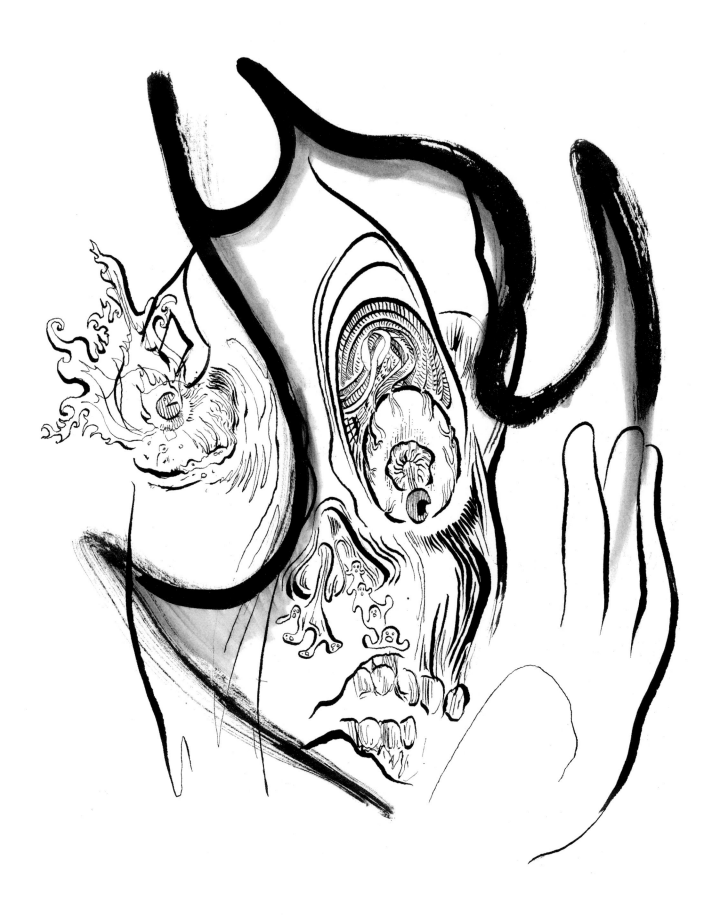

INSIDE THE ALLIGATOR LOUNGE
tony there's two of them
Look

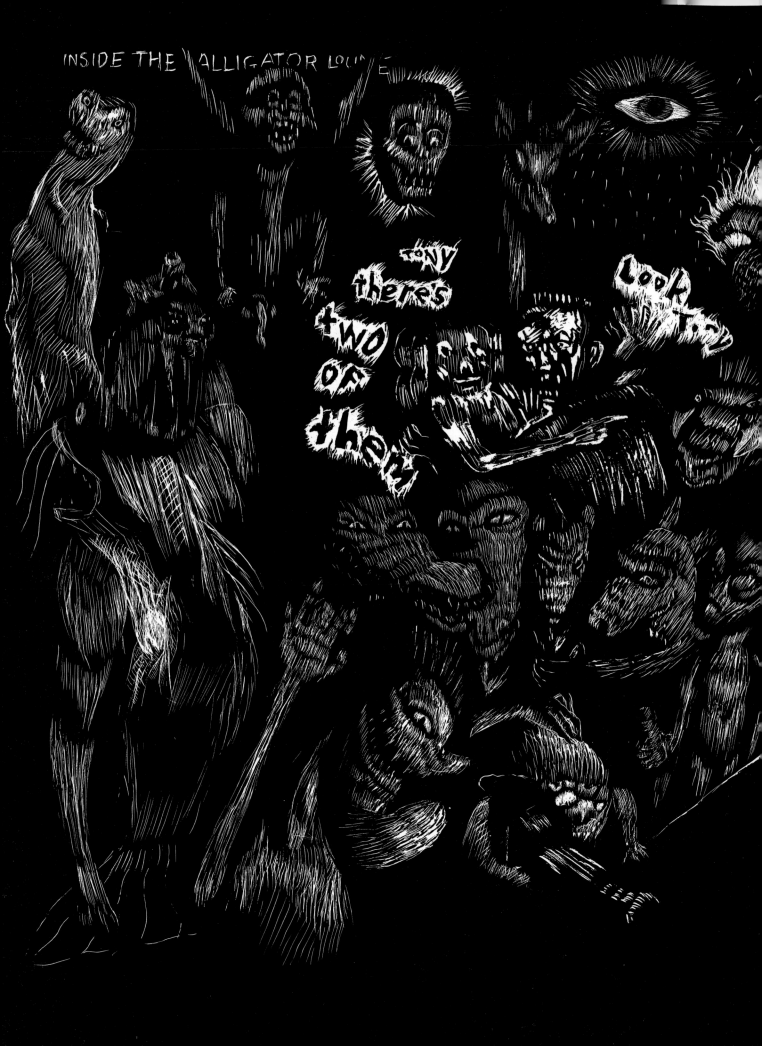

HEY GROUP HUDDLE BACK-STAGE
That's him.
OH YEAH?
Shit.
It's those two guys who molested me or whatever.
If Tim sees them he'll FREAK.
FUCK, FUCK, FUCK.
TREVOR
KIMBER-LY
The guy slobber-ing all over the blonde woman.

BACKSTAGE:
KISS
ADAM AND THE ANTS
Jam
RAMONES
X
CLASH
GOOD LUCK KIM
PLAY BILL
TALKING HEADS
SPECIALS
GALAXIE 500
MADNESS
PISTOLS
MINUTE MEN
WALL OF VOODOO RULE!
THEY suck! You KNOW who RULES?
E.L.O. ← They suck! but O.M.D. RULE!
BULLSHIT! THE BEST ACRONYMED BAND WAS B.T.O.!!!
NO WAY N.R.B.Q.
FUCK YOU! K.G.R.
CAT NIP
The 3 O'clock RULE
OKAY, DUDES, THIS IS IT. MAKE OR BREAK, MTV OR OBLIVION.
Maybe I should whip out my dick onstage.
DEVAN?!
BORN TO PARTY
WHO LOVES YA BABY?
Yeah, I'll hold out the magnifying glass.
OKAY!
LET'S DO IT!

TREVOR.
Yeah? Oh, you want an autograph? Uh, okay, but it has to be, uh quick 'cos
I'M... A FRIEND OF...
Tim's.
oh cool, he made it. Where is he?
LOOK, I... SOMETHING'S HAPPENED AND...
I don't know... how...
uh oh. What? Shit don't tell me. No wait
tell me.
NO WAIT DON'T TELL ME
okay, tell me.

HELLO, LOS ANGELES! I'M JED THE FISH FROM THE WORLD FAMOUS KROQ! KROQ, IN ASSOCIATION WITH THE ALLIGATOR LOUNGE, IS PROUD TO PRESENT ONE OF THE MOST TALKED ABOUT BANDS OF 1993–.
DOGSTAR!
BUT BEFORE THEY COME ON, HERE'S A LOCAL ACT. NEVER HEARD OF THEM MYSELF, BUT I MET THEM BACKSTAGE AND THEY'RE A REALLY NICE GROUP OF KIDS. SO GIVE THEM A WARM KROQ WELCOME
HORROR HOSPITAL!
WE WANT KEANU! WE WANT KEANU! WE WANT KEANU

THE OLD MAKE-EM-WAIT-FOR THE SINGER TRICK.
IT'S BEEN DONE.

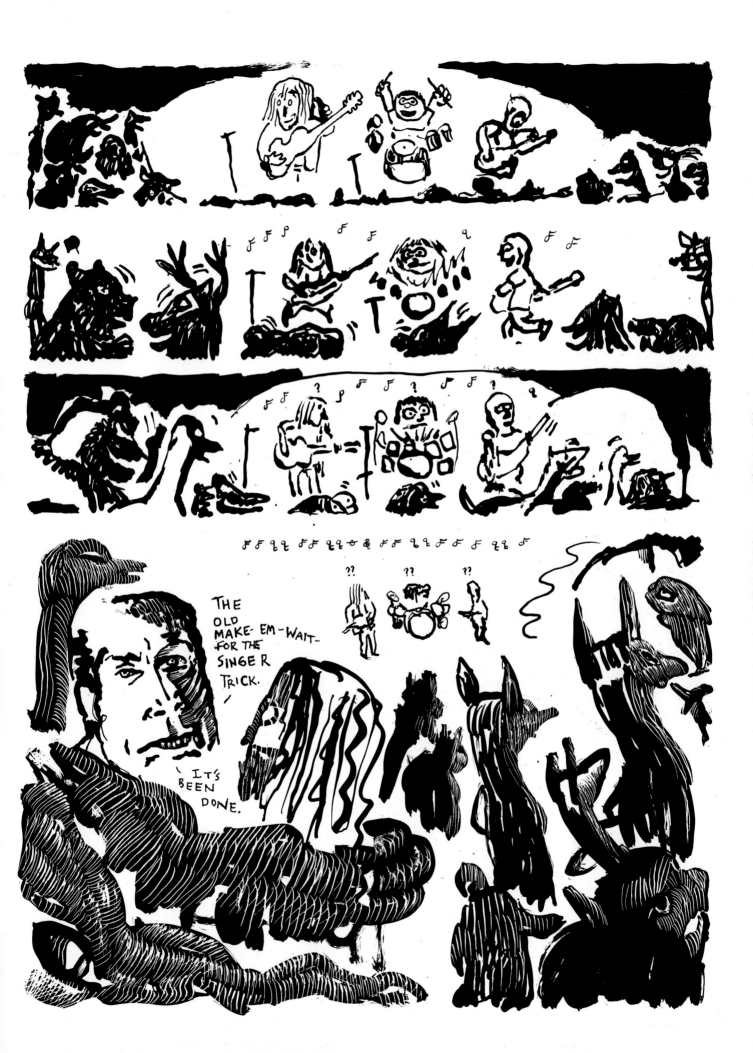

Fuck
Fuck
Fuck

I
LOOK
JUST

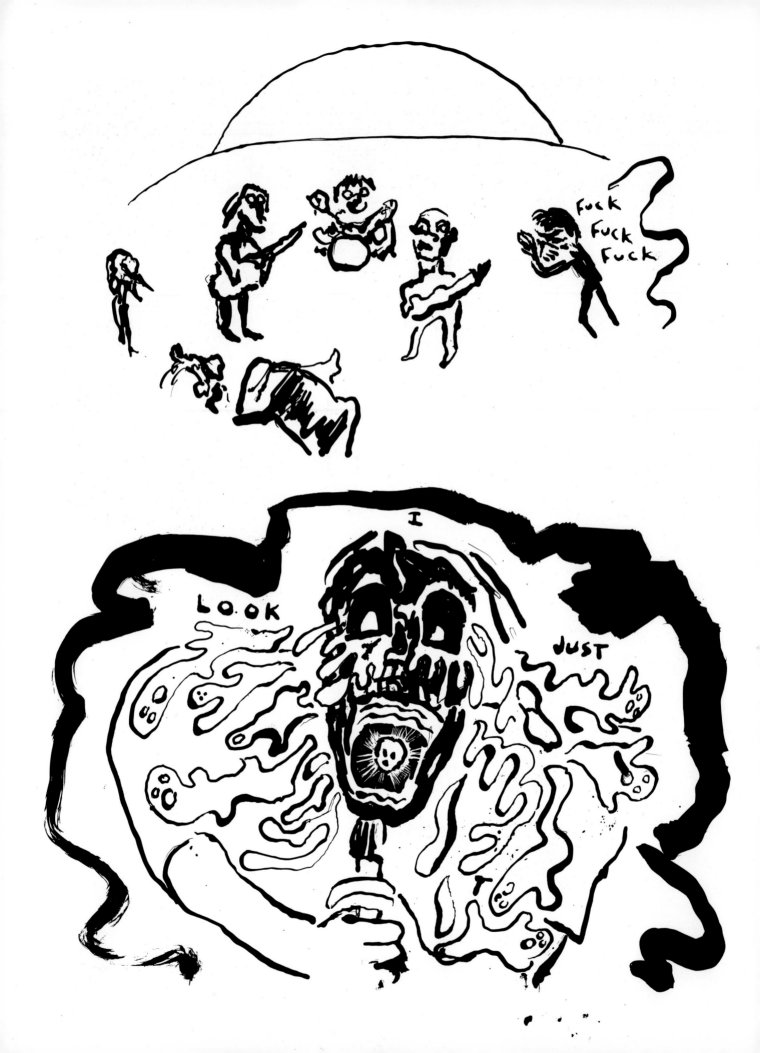

STOP FUCKING PLAYING

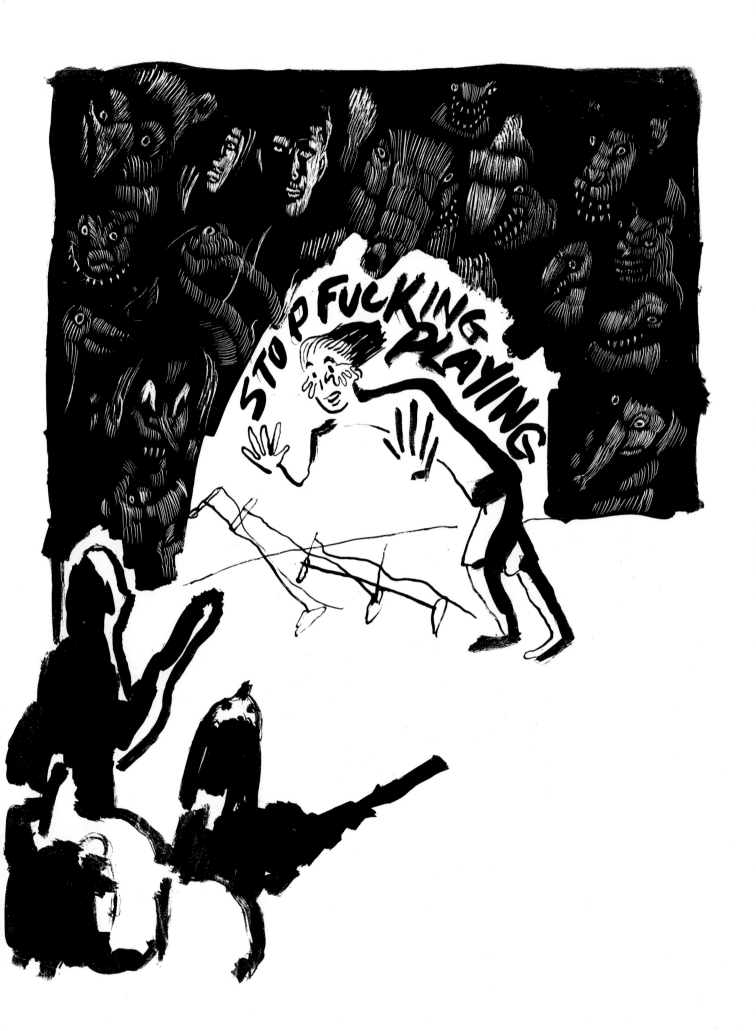

Look I JUST FOUND OUT

SOME THING I CAN'T

MY BOYFRIENDS

DEAD.

OH FUCK. HE JUST DIED IN A CAR ACCIDENT, AND

FAG
FAG!
OH, BOO HOO!
WHO CARES?
WHO CARES
OH BOO HOO!

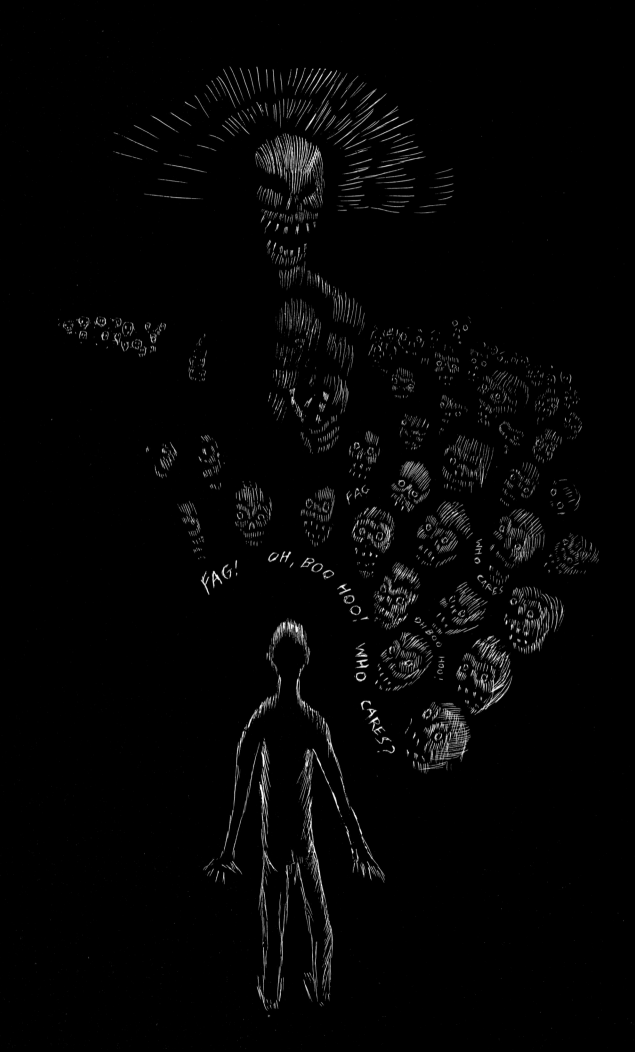

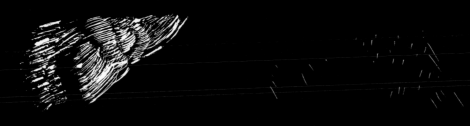

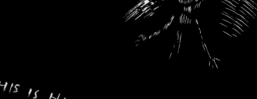

...AND I HATE ALL YOU FUCKING...

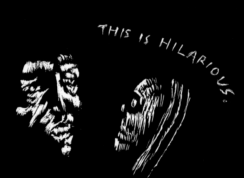

THIS IS HILARIOUS.

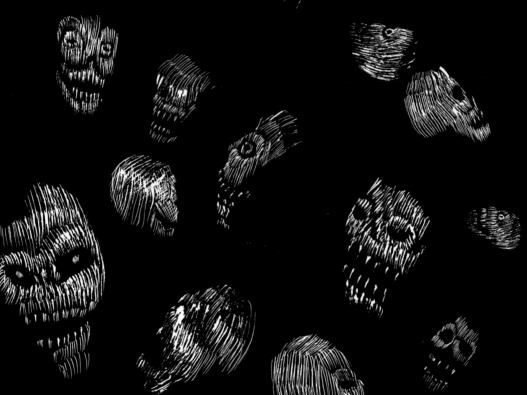

START THE SONG!! SHIT!

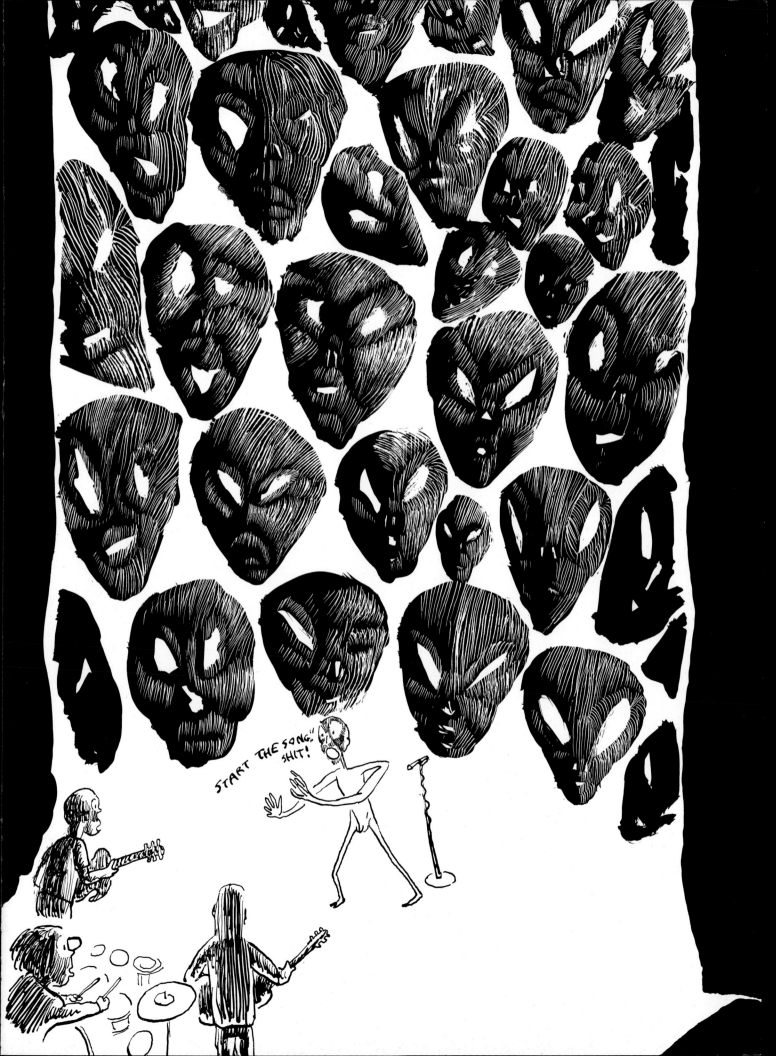

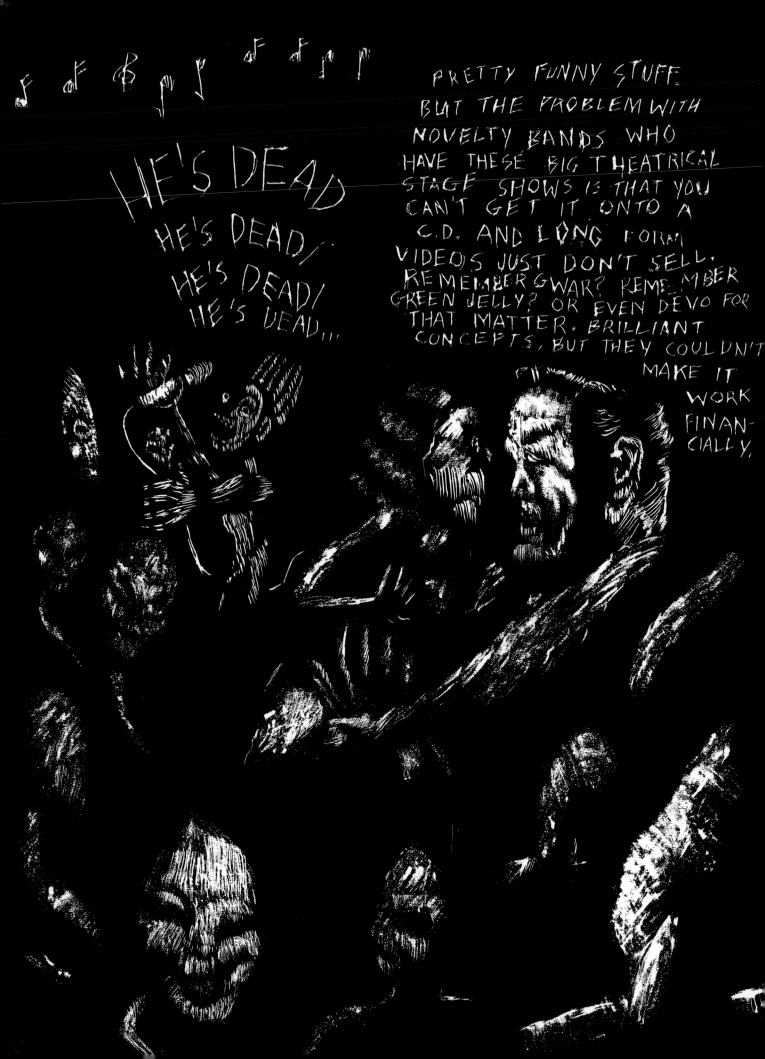

HE'S DEAD

HE'S DEAD/

HE'S DEAD/

HE'S DEAD...

PRETTY FUNNY STUFF
BUT THE PROBLEM WITH
NOVELTY BANDS WHO
HAVE THESE BIG THEATRICAL
STAGE SHOWS IS THAT YOU
CAN'T GET IT ONTO A
C.D. AND LONG FORM
VIDEOS JUST DON'T SELL.
REMEMBER GWAR? REMEMBER
GREEN JELLY? OR EVEN DEVO FOR
THAT MATTER. BRILLIANT
CONCEPTS, BUT THEY COULDN'T
MAKE IT
WORK
FINAN-
CIALLY.

WELL, THIS IS QUITE A DISAPPOINTMENT. THE COMEDY'S FAR TOO QUIRKY. IF YOU'RE GOING TO PARODY EDDIE VEDDER, YOU'VE GOT TO DO THE MOVES. THE CLIMBING OF THE AMPLIFIERS, THE SWAN DIVES INTO THE AUDIENCE. THIS IS TOO... PRECIOUS. AND THE SINGER IS A LOT LESS CUTE IN PERSON.
I'M STILL JOHNNY DEPP
HI I'M SUPPOSED TO BE TOM CRUISE DRESSED INCOGNITO
I NEVER TOLD HIM ANYTHING

I
WANT
TO

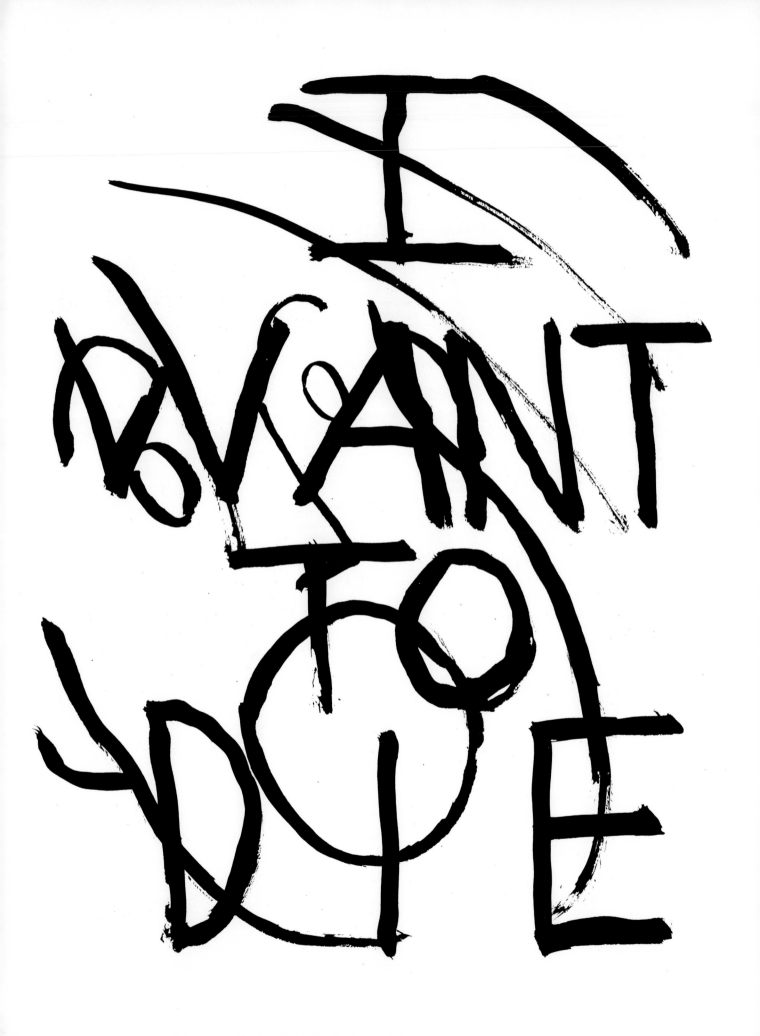

I WANT TO DIE

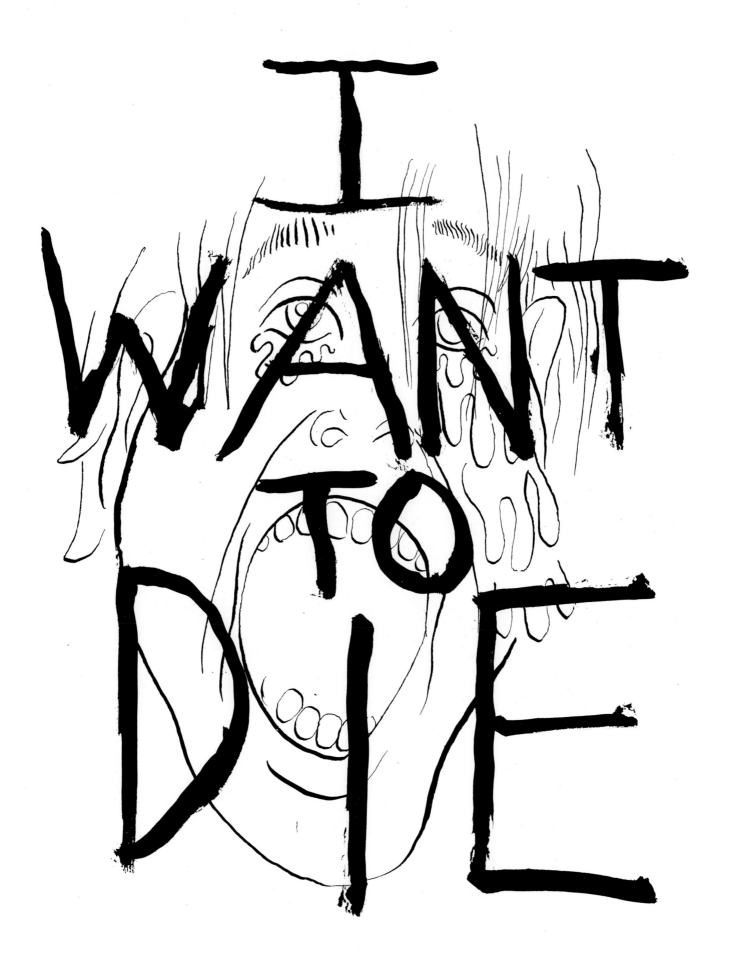

I
WANT
TO
DIE

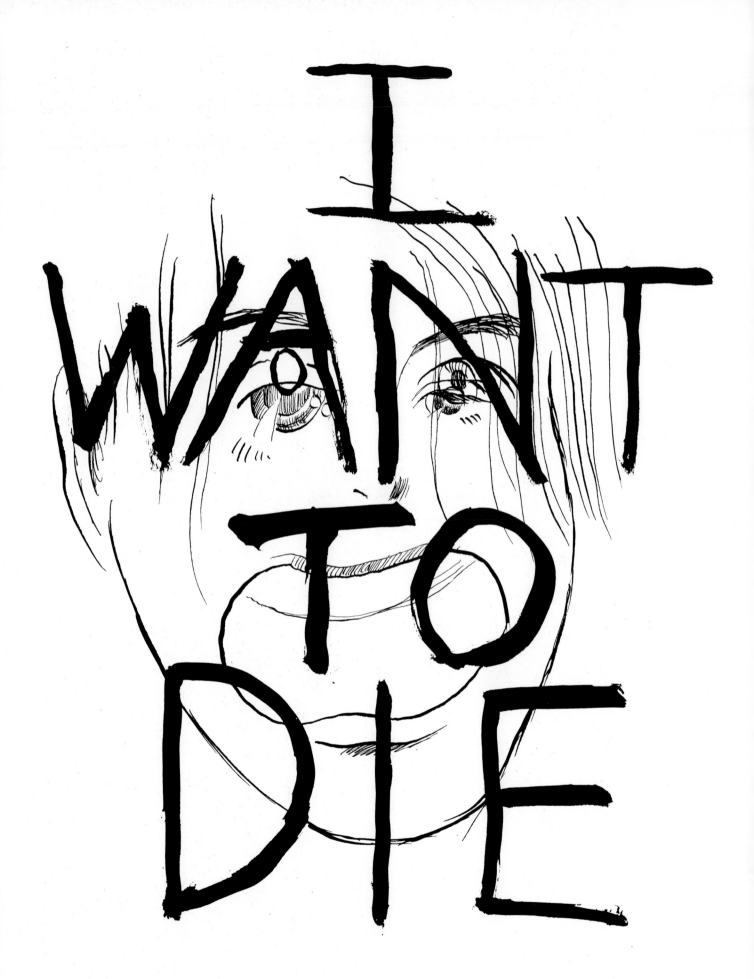

WHAT A SHAME. OH WELL I THINK I'VE SEEN ENOUGH.

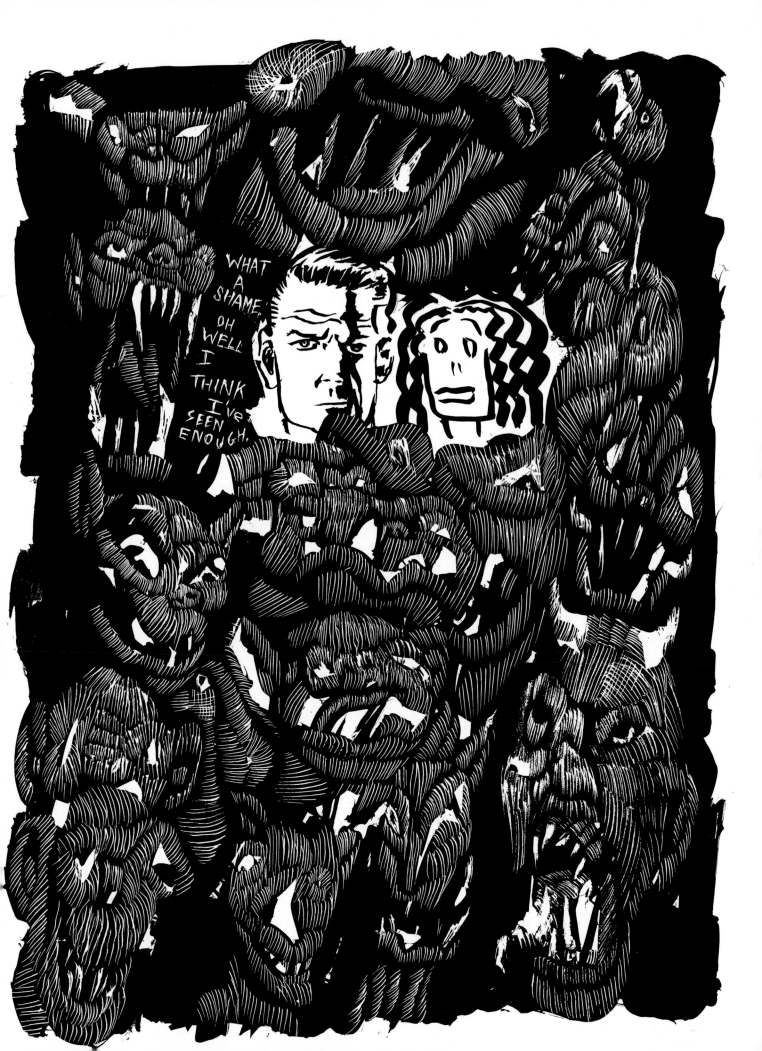

ARE YOU READY? I THINK WE
CAN JUST MAKE IT BEFORE IT CLOSES.
I'D RATHER BE FISHING

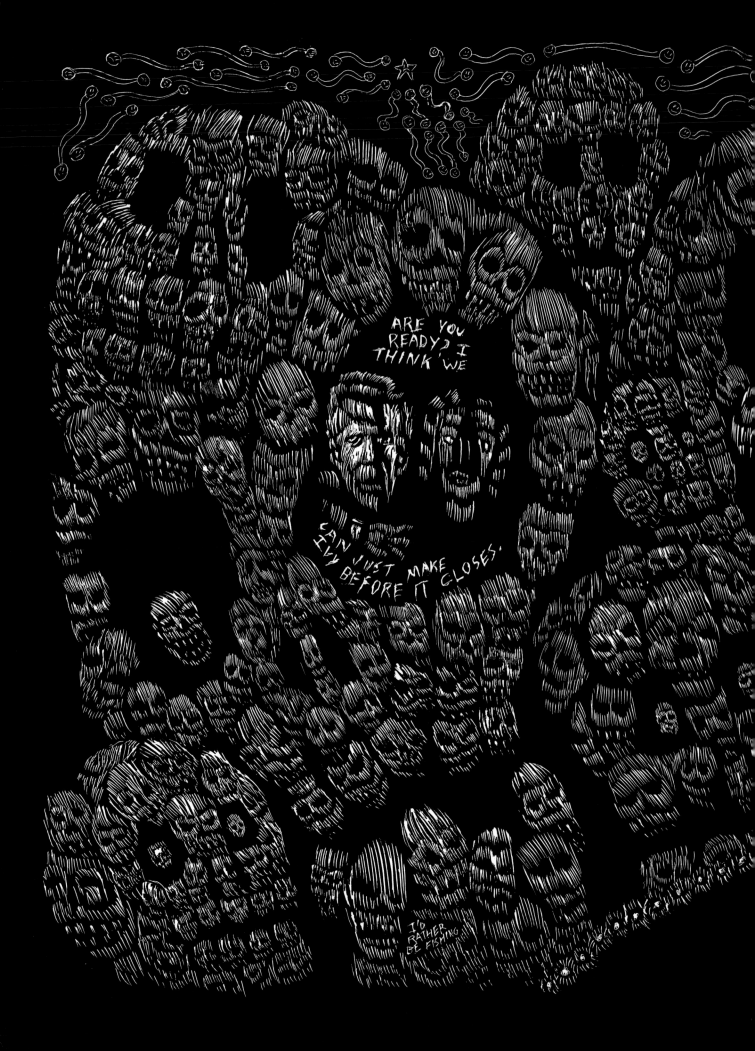

I WANT TO DIE

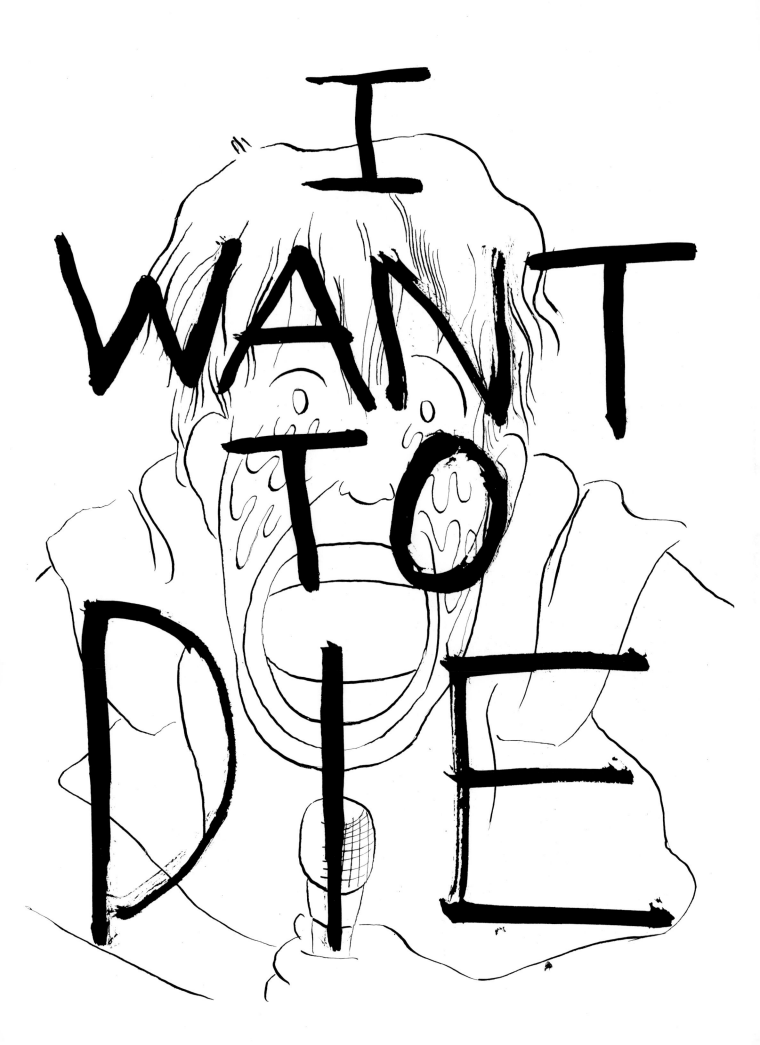

I WANT TO DIE

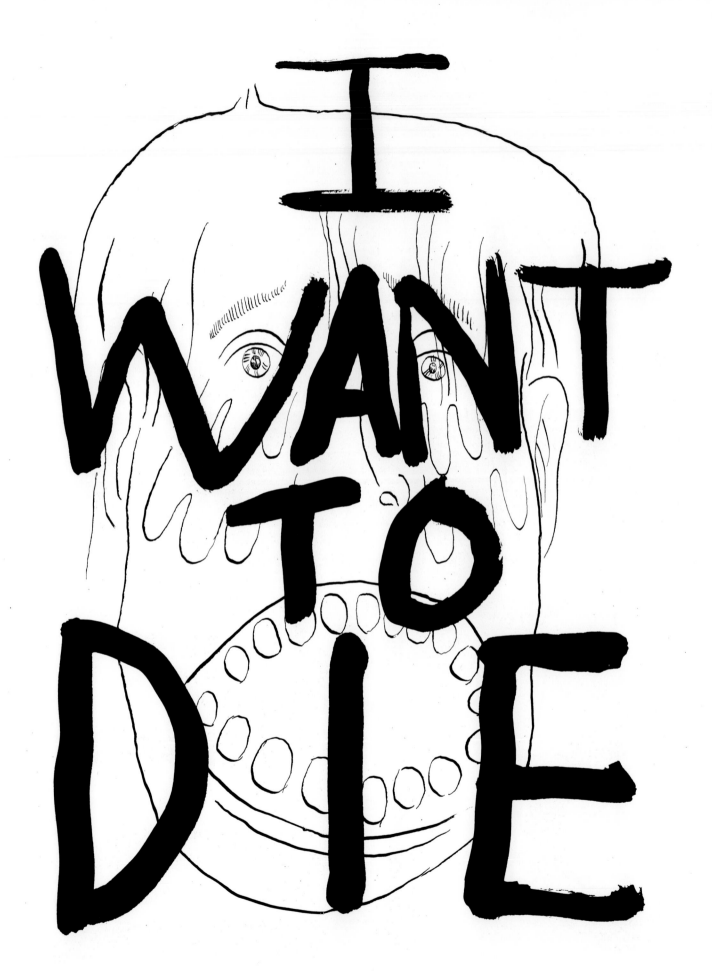

I
WANT
TO
DIE

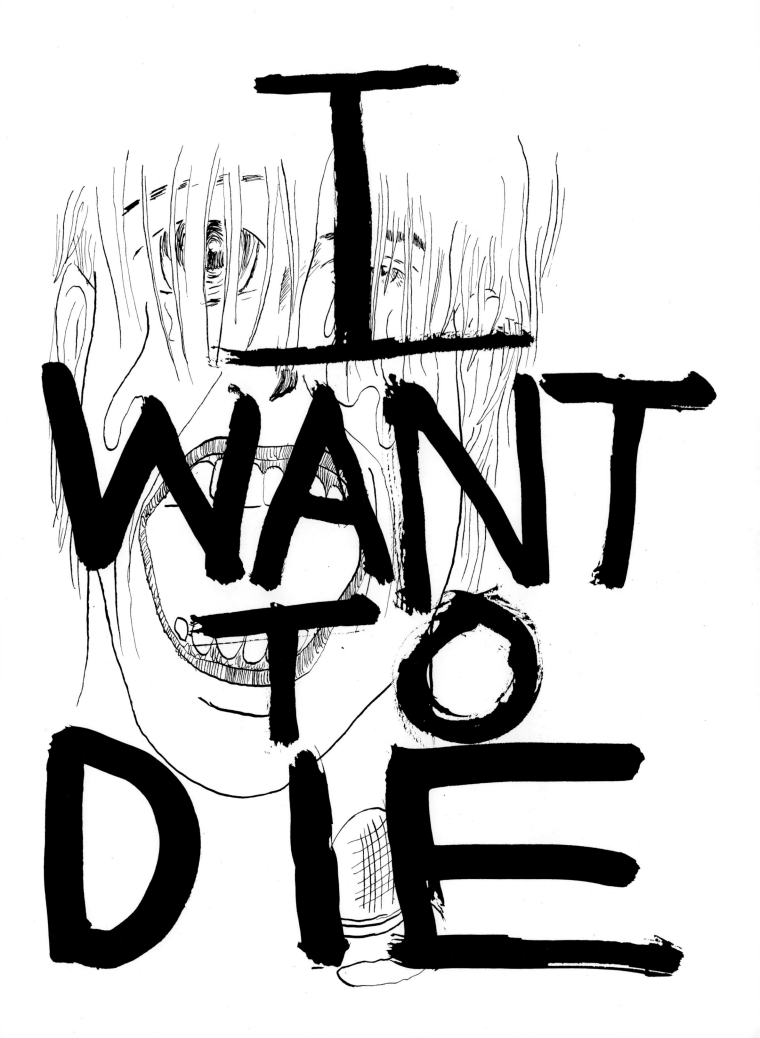

HILARIOUS.

I WANT TO DIE

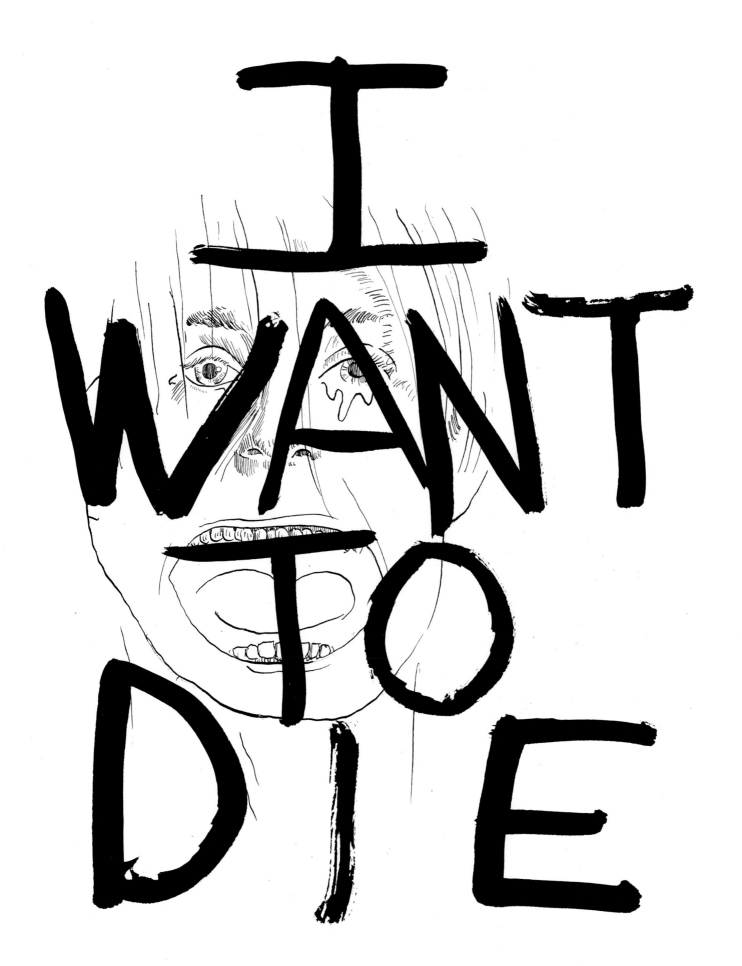

MY PLEASURE, KID.

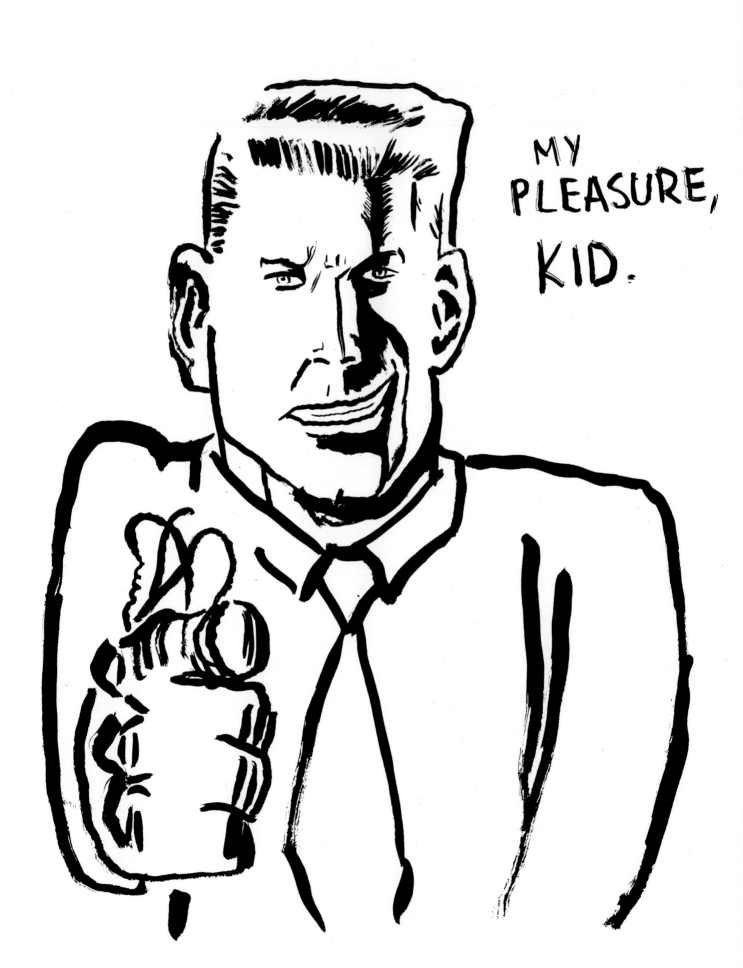

BANG.

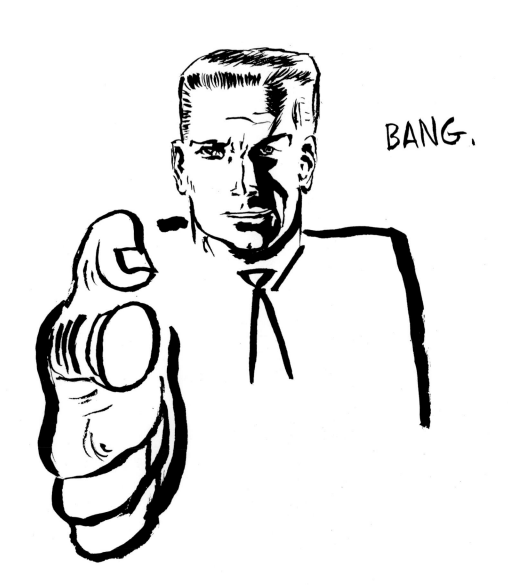

CATALOG

Angry Women in Rock, Vol. 1

Edited by Andrea Juno

Angry Women in Rock, Volume I takes up where the best-selling *Angry Women*—a book that inspired a whole generation of young women who have redefined feminism for themselves—left off. Thirteen female musicians and producers, ranging in experience from the established to those of the young underground, discuss their views on politics, sexuality, creativity, violence, authority, feminism, corruption and exploitation in the music industry, and many other topics.

Angry Women in Rock, Vol. I is the first definitive map to a rapidly developing, but still wild, pop culture terrain. The women interviewed, with rare honesty and candor, cover such diverse topics that the book has tremendous appeal even to those who don't know or care much about rock music, and serves as an inspiration to both women *and* men.

"I always laugh at that question, 'What's it like to be a woman in rock?' I don't have any memory of being a man in rock, so I have nothing to compare it to!"
—Valerie Agnew, 7 Year Bitch

"You get hot and you take off your shirt. Men have been doing that onstage forever. So why is it not okay for us to do? I'm playing, I'm hot, I'm taking off my shirt!" **—Lynn Payne, Tribe 8**

JUNO BOOKS
ANGRY WOMEN IN ROCK
Volume One
CHRISSIE HYNDE
JOAN JETT
7 YEAR BITCH
RIOT GRRRLS
PHRANC
TRIBE 8
JARBOE Swans
FANNY
CANDICE K Records
KENDRA SMITH
NAOMI YANG Galaxie 500
KATHLEEN HANNA Bikini Kill
BETTINA RICHARDS Thrill Jockey Records
LOIS
FROM THE FORMER CO-PUBLISHER OF RE/SEARCH PUBLICATIONS
RE SEARCH

FEATURING: Chrissie Hynde ♦ Joan Jett Kathleen Hanna (Bikini Kill) **♦ 7 Year Bitch Jarboe** (Swans) **♦ Tribe 8** (the all-dyke punk band) **♦ Bettina Richards** (Thrill Jockey Records) **♦ Kendra Smith ♦ Naomi Yang** (Galaxie 500) **♦ Phranc** (the "All-American Jewish Lesbian Folksinger") **♦ Candice Pedersen** (K Records) **♦ June Millington** (of Fanny, the '60s hard-rocking, all-female band)

Angry Women

The critically-acclaimed book that influenced a whole generation of women in which 16 cutting-edge performance artists unleash their creative visions and cultural vengeances.

RE SEARCH
ANGRY WOMEN

"These women are definitely dangerous models of subversion!"
—*MONDO 2000*

FEATURING: Kathy Acker ♦ Susie Bright Karen Finley ♦ Diamanda Galás ♦ bell hooks ♦ Avital Ronell ♦ Holly Hughes Sapphire ♦ Linda Montano ♦ Kerr & Malley Annie Sprinkle ♦ Wanda Coleman ♦ Valie Export ♦ Carolee Schneeman

"This is hardly the nurturing, womanist vision espoused in the 1970s. The view here is largely pro-sex, pro-porn, and pro-choice. Art and activism are inseparable from life and being." —*The Village Voice*

Incredibly Strange Music, Vol. 2

RE SEARCH
Incredibly Strange
Music
Volume II

"The bible of lounge is *Incredibly Strange Music.*"
—*Newsweek*

"Fans of ambient, acid jazz, even industrial rock, will find the leap back to these genres an easy one to make." —*Rolling Stone*

CATEGORIES INCLUDE: Exotica-ploitation ♦ Outer Space ♦ Brazilian Psychedelic ♦ Singing Truckdrivers Yodeling ♦ Sitar-Rock ♦ Religious Ventriloquism ♦ Moog ♦ and much more!

ALSO AVAILABLE . . .

Incredibly Strange Music, Vol. 2 CD

RE SEARCH
Incredibly Strange
Music

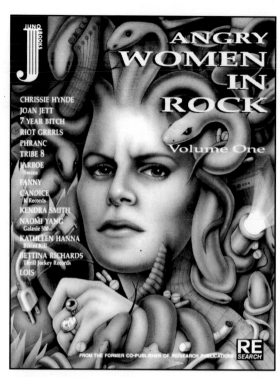

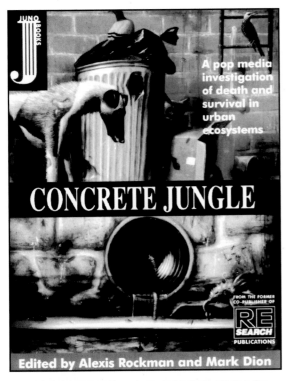

Edited by Alexis Rockman and Mark Dion

Concrete Jungle

A multi-media investigation of death and survival in urban ecosystems
AVAILABLE OCTOBER 1996

As the century comes to a close, editors Alexis Rockman, Mark Dion and other contributors take on new and innovative perspectives for exploring ecology and human interaction with nature and animals. This book runs the gamut from hilarious to foreboding end-of-the millennium eco-facts, and is a pop media investigation of what happens to organisms as they adapt to and thrive in our urban ecosystem. Packed with provocative photos and informative explorations of the city, *Concrete Jungle* approaches ecology in a contemporary fashion with irony and dark-edged humor.

In addition to documenting urban survivors, the book will include an interview with the Rat Catcher of New York City; a photo essay on roadkill (complete with recipes); a look at sci fi, exploitation and Hollywood films following the "nature runs amuck" theme, and much more.

COMING IN 1997 FROM JUNO BOOKS

◆ **SEX, STUPIDITY AND GREED:**
The Underbelly of the American Movie Industry
A revealing look at the tricks and tragedies of the American movie machine.

◆ **ANGRY WOMEN IN ROCK, VOL. 2**
An explosive continuation of the Angry Women series.

The RE/Search Guide to Bodily Fluids

By Paul Spinrad

CHAPTERS INCLUDE:
Mucus ◆ Menstruation ◆ Saliva Sweat ◆ Earwax ◆ Vomit Urine ◆ Flatus ◆ Feces ◆ and much more.

ORDER BY MAIL OR PHONE
Phone: 212-807-7300
Fax: 212-807-7355
JUNO BOOKS
180 Varick Street, 10th Floor
New York, NY 10014
Please call M-F, 10 a.m. to 6 p.m., EST

Name: _____
Address: _____
_____
_____
Phone: _____

Please indicate if you would like to be added to our mailing list, or send a SASE for a complete catalog.

I am paying by:
☐ Check or Money Order (payable to Juno Books)
☐ Credit Card (circle one): **VISA   MC**
VISA/Mastercard #   Exp. Date

Signature: _____

◆ ORDER FORM ◆

TITLE	QUANTITY	TOTAL
Angry Women in Rock, Vol. 1 ($19.95)		
Concrete Jungle ($19.95)		
Horror Hospital Unplugged ($18.95)		
R/S #13: Angry Women ($18.99)		
R/S #15: Incredibly Strange Music, Vol. 2 ($17.99)		
Incredibly Strange Music, Vol. 2 CD ($12.99)		
R/S # 16: Guide to Bodily Fluids ($15.99)		
Payment in U.S. dollars only. Allow 6-8 weeks for delivery.	**SUBTOTAL**	
	NY Residents (add 8.25% sales tax)	
	Domestic Shipping & Handling (first item $4, each additional item $1)	
	TOTAL DUE	

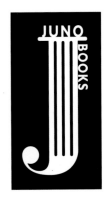

JUNO BOOKS

CATALOG

THE END

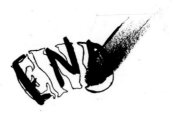

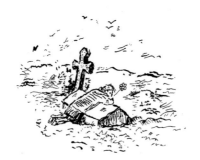

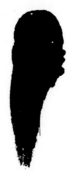